Scrapbook of a Year and a Day:

January 19, 2020 to January 20, 2021

by Karen Molenaar Terrell

PROLOGUE

Election Night, 2016

The voice said, "Trust. Everything is happening as it needs to happen. Don't be afraid. Trust."

January 18, 2020

Dad is in bed. His eyes are closed. He's very still, but I see his chest moving. He's still with us. I lean over and kiss his forehead and say into his ear, "Hi Daddy. It's Karen."

(There's no response at first. Then his eyes open and he looks at me.)

Dad: (Weakly.) Karen.
Karen: I love you, Daddy.
Dad: (I can feel the effort he's making to mumble the words.) Ah uv you.
Karen: (Smiling at Dad - my heart filled with tenderness.) You old mountain goat. (That's what Mom had always called Dad - and it comes to me - out of the blue - to call him that. Dad smiles at me. And now I find myself singing to him - that old Jeannette McDonald-Nelson Eddy song that he and Mom used to sing to each other...) When I'm calling you-ooh-ooh-ooh-ooh-ooh-ooh... (I see Dad perk up a little. I get this sense that Mom is calling to him.)

We don't say much after this. I stay for a while, stroking Dad's forehead, and watching "Maverick" on Dad's television. Every now and then Dad opens his eyes and checks to see if I'm still there. Eventually he falls back to sleep. I leave to go home and fetch my husband and son for a return visit. When I arrive home and describe Dad's condition, the husband and son immediately let me know they're with me and we go back to Dad's house.

We enter Dad's room and approach the bed. He's sleeping. We pull up three chairs and watch him for a while. His foot is moving back and forth. I approach Dad's bed.

Karen: Hi, Daddy. It's Karen. And Andrew is here. And Scotty.

(Dad opens his eyes and looks at me.)

Karen: I love you, Daddy.

(Dad's eyes are locked on mine and he nods his head at me once, twice. An affirmation. I nod back at him. He reaches up and holds my arm and squeezes it gently. I hold his hand and squeeze. He squeezes my hand back.)

Karen: Here's Andrew, Daddy.

(Andrew sits close to his grampa. This is his time with Grampa. Love is exchanged. This time belongs to them and it's not mine to share in words.)

Karen: And here's Scotty.

(Scott grips Dad's hand and receives a strong grip in return. They both grin at each other. Male bonding.)

We all feel when it's time to leave and let Dad get back to the business of sleeping. I get up and kiss Dad's forehead and tell him I love him. Scott says his good byes. Andrew is the last to leave - he gets a strong good bye handshake from his grandfather before he leaves him to sleep.

January

Washington State Dept. of Health:
For immediate release: January 21, 2020 (20-006)
Contacts: Lisa Stromme Warren, Washington State
Department of Health
Heather Thomas, Snohomish Health District

OLYMPIA– Today the Washington State Department of Health (DOH) confirmed a case of 2019 novel coronavirus (2019-nCoV) in a Snohomish County resident. While the risk to the general public is low, DOH is working with the Centers for Disease Control and Prevention (CDC) and Snohomish Health District to identify and contact all those who may have come in contact with the confirmed case. These individuals will be monitored for fever and respiratory symptoms.

"As our team of experts partners with infectious disease specialists locally, nationally and around the globe to learn more about the 2019 novel coronavirus, our first priority remains public safety," said Washington State Secretary of Health, John Wiesman. "We believe the risk to the public is low. And as this situation evolves, we will continue to communicate with the CDC, Snohomish County and the public."

Looking for My Obituary

Whoahhh...

I've always been fascinated by obituaries - I love reading about peoples' lives - where they lived, what they did, how they spent their time here, what adventures they had, what talents and gifts, who they loved and what other lives they touched while they were here. And... maybe this will tell you where I am right now... I just typed in my name to see if I could find my own obituary and read it. Yeah. I think it is time for me to go to bed...

Alrighty. Carry on then...

William W. writes: *As far as I know, I'm the only person with my name in the United States!*

Karen writes: *I'm pretty sure I'm the only Karen Molenaar Terrell in the whole wide world. Possibly the universe. Maybe.*

Elizabeth E. Fisher writes: *Let's hope!!*

Karen writes: *Very funny, Liz.*

January 19, 2020

Andrew spent the night. This morning I drove him back to Bellingham. As we reached the top of the hill, just before we exited onto I-5, a coyote suddenly trotted across the road in front of us. I'd never seen a coyote so close! It took both Andrew and I by surprise. We both said, simultaneously, "Whoaaah!"
Karen: That was magic!
Andrew: Yeah, it was!

I dropped Andrew off at his home and headed for the boardwalk. I planned on getting in a quick walk before heading back down and visiting with Dad. It seemed like it'd been a really long time since I'd had a walk along the boardwalk, breathed in the salt air, communed with the birds. When I reached the boardwalk I checked my phone messages and found Gwen had texted me...

9:16
Gwen B.: Not so good this morning.
9:26
Karen: Thank you for letting me know. I'll be there in a couple hours.
9:40
Gwen B.: You might want to make some calls and let your brothers know.

As I started on my walk I got a call from Amanda...
10:08
Amanda B.: I think it's going to happen soon.

Karen: I'm walking in Bellingham. Should I come right now?
Amanda B.: No. Finish your walk. It should be fine.
Karen: Thank you, Amanda. I'll be there soon.

I walked down the ramp and to the boardwalk, and looked out across the bay. The lighting was amazing - the sky and water seemed to be glowing. I felt close to Dad in that moment. (Later I learned that - in that same moment - Andrew had come down to the bay, too, and was looking across it - feeling touched and inspired by the beauty, and feeling close to his grampa.)

It wasn't until I was almost done with my walk and on my way back to the car that I thought to check my messages again. Gwen had sent me one at 10:17...
Gwen B.: You might want to come now.

I called Gwen to let her know I was on my way.

11:00
I was in Rosalita, driving to Dad's home, listening to Tracy Spring sing through my CD player - she was singing the song that comforted me through Mom's passing - that was comforting me now...

"All things pass
Of this I am sure
Love and Music will endure
And when I'm gone
Remember the song
Remember how I loved..."

My car phone cut through the music and I answered it.

Karen: Hello?

Krista from Hospice: Is this Karen?

Karen: Yes.

Krista: Are you almost to the home?

Karen: Yes, I should be there in 20 minutes. Is he still with us?

Krista: (Pause.) No. (This was not the answer I expected to hear. How many times before had we thought it was the end? And how many times had Daddy rallied? It seemed almost impossible to me that he hadn't rallied this time, too.) He passed peacefully. He was surrounded by love. We were all telling him how much we loved him.

Karen: (I felt myself still inside.) Thank you so much, Krista. I'm almost there. (The phone call ended. The music came back on. I found myself sobbing.) Oh, Daddy!

"Sing to me as I go
Soft and low
I no longer need to breathe
I am free..."
- Tracy Spring

January 20, 2020

Dad and Moz: Together again.

Daddy (Dee Molenaar) passed away yesterday morning. I guess some part of me felt that if we didn't announce his death, it wouldn't be real. I actually found myself going to Dad's page on Wikipedia to see if a death date was listed, yet – and when it wasn't listed I figured that meant Dad hadn't really died – because Wikipedia knows everything, right?

I wasn't with Dad when he passed – I was walking on the boardwalk in Bellingham. But he was surrounded by the dear care-givers who took him into their home three years ago and loved him as family. Our whole family has been so blessed by the care shown Dad at Cedar Grove. Thank you, Gwen, Amanda, Megan, and Dietrich. I don't know what we would have done without your love and support the last three years.

I have felt the support and love of all of you, too. I might go into hiding for a little while – so if you don't hear from me, please don't take it personally. It's just me doing what I do. I love you all – each and every beautiful one of you. Thank you for joining Dad and I on our adventures together the last three years. We couldn't have asked for better adventure-comrades.

As Dad would say, "Berg heil!"
Karen

January 22, 2020

Mass shooting in Seattle tonight. Youngest son, Xander, lives in Seattle, near where the shooting happened. Times are dark.

January 23, 2020

I know those of you who have lost loved ones can relate to encountering those weird little things that make you tear up or catch your breath or find closure. Here are some of the weird little things I've encountered in the last few days:

- The day after Pop died - before I'd made any announcement and only family knew he was gone - when we still had his passing to ourselves - I had the foresight to take a picture of my computer screen after I'd done a google search for "Dee Molenaar." At 9:32 am on 1-20 Dad was still alive, according to the World Wide Web.

- Amanda called from Dad's home to let me know she'd found his watch sitting on the bathroom counter. Oh wow! Daddy loved looking at his watch - the time was always off by an hour and 12 minutes - but he didn't care. I think it grounded him in some way to know his watch was on his wrist.

- As I was watching the last little patch of snow melting on our front lawn I realized that - whoah! - that snow had fallen from the sky and onto our lawn while Daddy was still alive. It was a little piece of the world left from Dad's time. And it was melting fast...

- I brought Dad's will to the courthouse to get it filed there. Had to go through security to get to the County Clerk's office. Had to remove metal from my person. And there was Dad's watch on my wrist! I'd forgotten I'd put it on! I felt a little jolt as I took it off and put it in the bin.

- Decided to drive the country back roads on my way home from the courthouse. Driving on roads I used to drive with Dad. Alone for the first time in days. I felt my face relax - felt it crumple up - and then there were tears pouring down - sobbing. My driving buddy is gone. My old hiking buddy is gone. My daddy is gone. The world is a different place than it was a week ago. And whoah! I'm the oldest now - the oldest offspring - and no parents left to stand between what comes next, and me. But I'm not even a grown-up, yet, right? So. What is happening here...?!!

January 25, 2020

Took Dad on a drive today. We went for a walk along Padilla
Bay and we saw water and eagles and swans - oh my!

January 27, 2020

I was up early this morning and out on the road, looking for magic - and I didn't even have to go a mile from home before I found it! During the night a flock of trumpeter swans had flown into a neighbor's field. I discovered the swans just as the sun was rising over the hills, shining its rays through the clouds. Sunrise on swans. Pure beauty. Pure wonder.

Our dear friend, Jack Arends, came up and took us out for lunch today. It was so good to see him again! This is the first time we've seen him since Dad's passing and we had a lot of memories to share.

A.D.W. writes*: Such a holy time already filled with love. Our hearts are with you and your family. I remember feeling like the leading edge of the generation when mom died. Like, it's all up to me and sibs now. My dog died a year ago today. I remember thinking that way about the snow. Tell tale signs he was still in the world. Love.*

Cassie D. writes*: Thank you for including us in your dad's journey, Karen. I truly feel like I know him. I am sending you all the love and light, my friend.*

Sandy R. writes*: I am so very sorry. Thank you for taking us along for the travels with him. He was a very blessed man!*

Cari Hornbein writes*: I am up way past my bedtime and I thought I'd check Facebook before turning in. I am so so sorry to hear about your dad. Sending lots of love.*

Peggy Bissell writes*: "Though loved ones are lost, love is not." (Dylan Thomas) Your journey of love with your dad has been a gift to all of us. And that journey will go on. Please know we are thinking of you, heart and soul, with lots of love. The love continues...*

Paul Swortz writes*: Much love to you, Scott, and the boys. It's been a pleasure and a privilege to read your accounts of your time together.*

David B. writes*: Berg Heil. Sending my deepest condolences to you, Scott and family, as you mourn your dad's death and* *celebrate his amazing life. Thank you for sharing your journey with us. I've enjoyed your very personal reflections. Peace...*

Karen Beckner writes: *Scott and Karen...thank you for sharing the amazing lives of Moz and Dee with us over the years. May you Rest In Peace as you remember they are together again now and you have the love and support of a huge community of friends and family. What a gift for all of us... love and peace to you. Hugs.*

Theresa B. writes: *Thank you for sharing the story of your father. I am sorry for your loss, but like to think he is reunited with your mother and his climbing comrades. He was a great man and did us all proud. Berg heil.*

Susanne K. writes: *The loving arms of the community are wrapped around you Karen. Thankful for the adventures you shared with us.*

Dawn B. writes: *Oooh sweetie, my heart dropped when I read this. Your stories have been such a blessing and because of you he lives on in all our hearts. Holding you close.*

Peg S. writes: *Karen, I am so sorry for your loss. Take time to take care of yourself now.*

Taraleen writes: *Karen, I can't imagine a better, more supportive way for your dad to exit this life. I have been in awe of the beautiful relationship, the unending patience, and the deep love you shared with him, but also with us, through your stories. Here's a big virtual hug. I have never seen nor known someone with such a natural gift for really showing up, being there, loving. Thank you for sharing this journey with us and please continue to reach out. We all adore and admire you.*

Jessie N. writes: *All my love and the biggest hug to you. Thank you for sharing every story of him - it's warmed our hearts more than you know.*

Jeff Chase writes: *Bless you and your family, and thank you.*

Mary Beth writes: *So much love coming your way, precious Karen - arms around you and prayers coming your way, honey. Your beautiful heart is so exquisitely generous in sharing all of your tender and interesting experiences with your incredibly wonderful dad. I feel so greatly enriched and blessed by all you have shared - so selflessly. All of our lives are richer for the deep love you both shared. I love you sweetie.*

Diana P. writes: *Aww Karen, I'm so sorry for the loss of your daddy! You two have (I'm not going past tense here) the most beautiful relationship. I've enjoyed your stories, but I think I've enjoyed the love you have for him more. Blessings to you.*

Pamm F. writes: *Oh Karen, you and your family are in my prayers. I know this is a time of deep reflection for you. I know all of the time you spent with your Dad will be a great comfort to you now. Take your time and be kind to yourself.*

Pam A. writes: *I'm so sorry to hear it, Karen. What a long, adventurous life he lived and I loved learning more about it through your stories.*

Diane L. writes: *A huge loss, not unexpected, but devastating nonetheless. We loved your Mom and Dad and will carry our special memories of them forever. Our love to you and the family and our heartfelt condolences.*

Kathy T. writes*: My heart is filled with love and thoughts of all the Dad and Karen adventures you so graciously shared with us. He led an amazing life and I feel privileged to have joined you on your journey these past few years.May your heart be filled with the love you shared with your Dad and the love we, your followers, are sending your way.*

Elizabeth E. Fisher writes*: I think this speaks of your father: "The encumbering mortal molecules, called man, vanish as a dream; but man born of the Great Forever, lives on, God-crowned and blest."- Mary Baker Eddy*

Janice M. writes*: Karen, deep breaths. Your dad was so special. From the bottom of my being, thank you. Thank you for sharing Moz and Dee with all of us. Now they are together again; remind yourself that when the ache becomes overwhelming. Take your time. Hold your loved ones tight. Hugs, Janice*

Karen Rippberger writes*: Dearest Karen. You and your parents are still traveling the road together; you're just holding hands a different way. Sometimes the new connection seems tenuous and it takes getting used to. But it is a strong, loving, compassionate, unbreakable grip and always has been. It is the same. Only different. And just as you love them, they love you. Take all the time you need to adjust to this new way of walking. Much love to you and yours.*

Linda F. writes*: Our love and sympathy on the passing of your dad, Karen. He was an exceptional man. What an incredible legacy he left behind, particularly in you*

Deb C. writes: *Karen, you cared for your father and took such great care of him. The stories you would write about your adventures driving around the countryside are priceless. I am thinking of you and your family. He will rest in peace and you will rest knowing he is with your mother again. They now get to live eternally together.*

Stephani Z. writes: *Oh, my dearest KT. Crying into my coffee this morning. You have made me feel like part of your family. While I never met your dad in person, I feel like I knew him. It's been a pleasure. And a joy. I hope you can feel my arms around you. Holding you close to my heart.*

Beverly C. writes: *I am so sorry. Even when we know this is coming, the moment puts us in shock. Oh, but what a wonderful loving life you and he have shared. Now he is reunited with your mom and they are yodeling together again. What joy must have been upon him as he saw his love waiting for him. You blessed us with your stories of his later years and your love for each other.*

Lori T. M. writes: *My sweet sis. I wish I could give you a big hug right now. I know that your parents are smiling down on you right now. Imagine the welcoming he got from your mom. I love you!*

Roland M. writes: *Oh Karen, I'm so sorry to read about your father's passing. Your family was blessed to have his presence until the ripe old age of 101. He certainly touched many of us in the wilderness appreciation, travel, and rescue community. We will all miss him. Most of all, he and Moz created a family together that will continue his legacy. May God bless you all.*

Debra M. writes: *I have been so deeply moved by your journey these past few years and now, with eyes brimming and spilling over, I am sending you a long-held hug...and not just for you, but for me, too. I love you, Karen, and I cannot be more sincere. Be well, sweetheart, and take your time coming into yourself again. xoxoxo*

Mary Ellen writes: *Just checking in to see how you're doing. You've been on my mind and in my heart and prayers. May you find peace and comfort in this difficult time. I always looked forward to your pictures and stories of visits with your dad. I never met him, but somehow he found a place in my heart. Hoping you are well. I am here for you, friend.*

Susan H. writes: *I'm saddened by the news of your dad's passing, Karen. But at the same time, I am so happy for the life he led and how peaceful and serene his end of life was. He was so lucky to have you there for all the drives and visits! Thanks for sharing those stories, Karen.*

Ben T. writes: *Sending you big hugs, my friend. Thank you for sharing so many wonderful stories of your dad. I feel like I knew him in person, and I feel all of this...every tear, every smile. All the love to you and your family.*

Peter Molenaar writes: *Thank you, Sis. Yes, first thought, they are together again. Now he knows where she is! No sadness, but joy for his wonderful, beyond description, freedom! He has plenty of wonderful souls to see again and mountains, even more grand than he knew here, to run around on. I imagine he is already pointing out and guiding other souls who have not yet been able to see them.*

David Molenaar writes: *I'm sure he's settling in with Moz and a yodel or two! I believe she stomped on the upstairs floor to come for dinner and he finally put his last brush stroke on another wonderful creation and bounded up the stairs to join her!*

Jack Arends writes: *Dee was a big deal, simply put. He was an early mountain guide on Mount Rainier who later wrote the authoritative book about that mountain (The Challenge of Rainier). He did that after climbing within 300 feet of the summit of K2 in 1953, and living to tell about it. In the 1960s, Dee was part of the team that climbed Mt. Kennedy in British Columbia with Robert Kennedy. And this was after Dee served in World War II and lettered in track at the UW.*

In the 1950s, Dee worked as a geologist with what is now the Washington Department of Natural Resources. It was there he and Colleen befriended Carol Arends, a secretary in the department, and her husband, John, a Tumwater shopkeeper. Their families remained friends for decades, after moves from Thurston to Kitsap Counties.

Bob S.A. writes: *It is with deep regret and profound sadness that I learned of the passing of a very special friend and personal hero. He was the last of his generation or, to use part of the title of one of his books; a dinosaur mountaineer. Happy to know he had a long life filled with adventures and surrounded by people who dearly loved him, and yet sad that an era has come to an end.*

Legendary Mountaineer, Artist and Author, Dies at 101

Anyone who has climbed Mount Rainier in the past 80 years has walked in the steps of Dee Molenaar.

Mr. Molenaar, who died of congestive heart failure on Jan. 19 at 101 years old, knew Rainier so well that he referred to it simply as "the mountain" where he hiked as a young man, a father, a National Park Service climbing ranger, a geologist and as an artist.

When he turned 100 in 2018, Mr. Molenaar sat at the base of Rainier in a wheelchair for one last visit with his old friend...

"A lot of climbers are competitive," said Karen Molenaar Terrell, Mr. Molenaar's daughter. "Who can get up there the fastest or the highest? But my father just loved being in the mountains and the friendships he made."

- Brodeur, Nicole. "Dee Molenaar: Legendary Mountaineer, Artist and Author, Dies at 101." Seattle Times, 7 February, 2020.

February

The U.S. Centers for Disease Control and Prevention will be testing for the coronavirus in people in five major cities who show up at clinics with flu-like symptoms but who test negative for the seasonal varieties.

If that testing shows the virus has slipped into the country in places federal officials don't know about, "we've got a problem," Dr. Anthony Fauci, director of the National Institute of Allergy and Infectious Diseases, told USA TODAY's Editorial Board Monday.

Short of that, Fauci says skip the masks unless you are contagious, don't worry about catching anything from Chinese products and certainly don't avoid Chinese people or restaurants...

"If you look at the masks that you buy in a drug store, the leakage around that doesn't really do much to protect you," he said. "People start saying, 'Should I start wearing a mask?' Now, in the United States, there is absolutely no reason whatsoever to wear a mask."

O'Donnel, Jayne. "Top disease official: Risk of coronavirus in USA is 'minuscule'; skip mask and wash hands."USA Today, 17 February, 2020.

Lambs Bouncing Around in the Fields

In a month there will be daffodils! And tulips will be budding! And lambs will be bouncing around in the fields!

Just thought I should point this out.

Alrighty. Carry on then...

February 1, 2020

We were shopping at Fred Meyer's today and I came upon a new version of "Monopoly" (the board game). This version is called "Monopoly: Cheater's Edition." It came out in June, 2018. Here's what the game is about: "Follow, bend or break the rules to win the Cheaters Edition of the Monopoly board game. Cheating is part of the game. Don't get caught. This Monopoly game includes a plastic handcuff unit that 'chains' cheating players to Jail space. Cheat cards encourage players to cheat and which cheat to attempt. Complete a cheat to get a reward; fail a cheat and pay the consequences."

And it strikes me that this new version of Monopoly is pretty representative of where our nation is right now...

February 2, 2020

Mom is gone. Dad is gone. Andrew's in Europe. Xander's in Seattle. I am in a weird place, my friends. There's nothing anyone needs to do about this. I just needed to share with someone - and you're the lucky someones.

February 3, 2020

You guys - something really weird and wonderful just happened - I just got a message on my author and photographer page from my old SEVENTH GRADE SOCIAL STUDIES TEACHER! From, like, 51 years ago!!! I had no idea this man was even still alive!!! And... I'm going to brag a little, okay? I don't know who else I can share this with. Here's what he said:

Dear Karen:

Sorry about your father. You were, he was, two people about whom I have always felt a tender feeling of great affection. There was, about you both, that sense of greatness mixed with humility and joy - the sense of people who know what they are doing is worth the struggle and its occasional less than always pleasant rewards. I was grateful for the story by Driscoll in the Tacoma Tribune about your father. I remember how inspired I was to meet him at a faculty-parent evening in Port Orchard - Lord knows how many years ago. What a great man, what a great family! Among the many treasures of a very poor teacher are the memories of having had in hand really wonderful students - and their parents - who taught me more than I taught them. Thank you!

john keliher

February 5, 2020

There is all kinds of crazy coming out tonight. Scroll down and
you'll see where I put my toe in the fray to explain that no, the
women senators didn't wear white because they are KKK
members - they wore white to honor the suffragettes... and...
crap. Our nation is in a lot of trouble, my friends.

February 20, 2020

Bloomberg: a gazillionaire who's been linked to sexual harassment allegations and who thought the search and frisk policy was great. What he has going for him is that if he were in a debate with the Republican candidate he could talk about being more "successful" and more wealthy and a better businessmen, and etc.

Buttigieg – what I like about him is his energy; his way of speaking; his background in the military service. I really wish he wouldn't show his ageism. I wish he had more experience at the national level.

Biden – he has the most experience working in the executive branch. He's likable and has a back story that's easy to sympathize with. But he's too connected to the old guard. He is not a visionary. He doesn't have the ability to inspire that others have.

Klobuchar – I like her a lot. I think she might be the best one of all of them at building consensus and working on compromise. But that scares me a little, too – I need to see that she can take a stand – that there are things she's not willing to compromise.

Sanders – he inspires me. He knows how to rouse us and lead us. He's smart. He has a quick sense of humor and knows how to use it to good effect. He stands his ground. He walks the walk. I love his wife. He's idealistic. He doesn't make compromises. This is the thing that also most concerns me – I'm not sure he'd be able to bring the two parties together and get things done. I don't think the Republican legislators would work well with him.

Warren – she knows what it's like to work hard to get where she is. I like that she was a special ed teacher. She's experienced what it is to be a woman in our society – and – I apologize for the sexism of this, but that's huge for me. She's been patronized. She's been condescended to. She was let go from her teaching job because she was pregnant – she knows what that feels like. She's idealistic – but she's also pragmatic. She stands up for the "little guy" and has done for all her life. I think she has ideas that would actually work – ideas that aren't just pie in the sky.

Anyone care to share their thoughts?

– Karen

February 21, 2020

I've been sort of dreading today all week. It's the third anniversary of Moz's passing today. Last night I found myself reliving in my thoughts the series of things that happened three years ago: Moz being brought to our home in an ambulance; Moz being wheeled on a stretcher through our front door; the hospice nurse coming over to show us how to care for Moz; the conversations Moz and I had; the uncertainty about what lay ahead. Did we have six months? Or less?

Last night I went to bed. Dreading. And I slept.

I slept right through the time of Moz's passing and beyond that – I think I got a full eight hours in! And when I woke up this morning there was a lightness to my heart. I felt joy.

I ended up at Lake Padden – did a quick walk around the lake – it was beautiful up there today. And I felt Moz and Dad with me.

And that's the thing, isn't it? We're never really separated from those we love! Never! The love is as real now as it was three years ago! The love's never died. All that's real never dies.

Just had to share.

I've Been Sick

Cassie D. writes: *I'm struggling with efficient communication with Mom's new caregiver. She's just informed me that she's not able to drop mom at the hospital for a scheduled procedure Friday morning. Is there any chance you might feel comfortable picking her up at home and dropping her at the hospital by 11 am on Friday?*

Karen writes: *Cassie, I'm so sorry! - I won't be able to do this on Friday - but I feel so honored that you thought of me. I've been sick - runny nose, coughing, sore throat, shivers, sleeping a lot - I don't want to risk the chance of making your mum sick - also, my mom's death anniversary is on Friday. I'm just not on top of things right now. I'm going to try to think of someone else who might be able to help you...*

March

Don't wear face masks to fend off the coronavirus, the World Health Organization says.

"There is no specific evidence to suggest that the wearing of masks by the mass population has any potential benefit. In fact, there's some evidence to suggest the opposite in the misuse of wearing a mask properly or fitting it properly," WHO executive director of health emergencies Mike Ryan said Monday.

The WHO says the only people who need masks are those who are already sick and those who are caring for the sick.

Ryan also cited the global shortage of medical supplies and the risk frontline workers are facing every day.

"The thought of them not having masks is horrific," Ryan said.

Voice of America. "WHO: Don't Wear Face Masks." March 30, 2020 (https://www.voanews.com/science-health/coronavirus-outbreak/who-dont-wear-face-masks)

What Is Good in This World

Here's a thought that's been really helpful to me in the last several years: We don't ever need to side with people - not with Trump or Pelosi or Obama or McCain, or whoever - we just need to side with Truth and Love. If I start there - with Truth and Love - everything else sort of falls into place after that. Is this path leading me towards Love - towards being kinder, more thoughtful, more selfless, more compassionate, more understanding of others? If not, then do not waste time with it. Does that road lead to Truth? Is it going to make me more honest? Will I still have my integrity intact at the end of that road? If not, then do not follow that road.

I'm thinking our only loyalty should be to what is good in this world - to what is kind and honest and selfless and decent and honorable.

And this concludes today's sermon.

Alrighty. Carry on then...

- Karen

Homesick for a Place That No Longer Exists

Today I felt an urge to drive to the old homestead
in Port Orchard and surprise the folks with a visit.
I imagined
the smile on Moz's face when she saw me
walk in the door.
I imagined
Dad scaling the stairs to greet me.
I imagined
taking a walk through the woods to the creek,
looking for new spring buds on the alders,
and squirrels scrambling through the cedars.

Feeling homesick
for a place that no longer exists.
– Karen Molenaar Terrell

March 2, 2020

Yesterday was a beautiful, perfect, heart-stretching day. Scotty and I drove to Seattle for a visit with Xander and Kyla - we walked through the arboretum together and ate at our favorite vegan restaurant, Araya's. Then back to Bow and a house concert at the incomparable Mary Ann's home with the equally incomparable Tracy Spring filling our hearts up with hope and joy and deep things from Soul.

Daffodils in the Wind

It was a beautiful and perfect day, but not in the way
that you probably imagine. The skies were grey,
the new daffodil blossoms bent over in the gusting
wind. It was a hot tea and zipped jacket day.
There was a sweet melancholy in my thoughts
as I drove by your old home, our old haunts,
and remembered the two of you, laughing and happy,
exploring your new hometown. There was no pain
in the sweet sadness. No tears. A gentle gladness
for the time I had with you here. It was a day to rent
"The Secret Garden" and watch young Mary learn
about hope and magic while a fire danced and burned
in the woodstove and a cat curled up on my lap for a nap.
.–Karen Molenaar Terrell

March 13, 2020

You can maybe tell a lot about people when they're at the
supermarket preparing for the Apocalypse. Where do I head
first? For the chocolate.

March 15, 2020

To Fred Meyer's shoppers and Hagen's shoppers, and the people I've passed on my walks on the Bellingham boardwalk – thank you so much for exchanging smiles with me in the last couple weeks! Everyone I've encountered has been kind and courteous and helpful. Thank you for laughing with me at the empty toilet paper shelves. Thank you for extending your elbows to me. I've heard stories of folks fighting over toilet paper, stock-piling hand sanitizers – I'd been a little concerned about virus vigilantes trying to lock people in a quarantine if they sneezed – but all I've encountered in the last few weeks has been unshakeable kindness. Maybe we have to keep our physical distance from each other – but isn't it cool that smiles can extend beyond six feet?!

Smiles are powerful things, my friends. Keep 'em coming!

March 16, 2020

So my son, Andrew, has been traveling through Europe since the end of January. He spent a few weeks on a sheep farm in Austria. Now he's at a horse therapy place in Germany. He plans to travel to the Netherlands in a week or two to visit an "art forest."

I just heard they're planning to close down borders between European nations there.

I am concerned.

I know. I am not being very Christianly Scientific. But I sure could use some prayerful thoughts. Anybody got anything?

March 17, 2020

Last week we cancelled the flight to Pittsburgh that we were going to take to see Scott's family because – duh! – right? We thought it might be cool to make our annual trek to Lincoln City, Oregon, instead. So we booked a couple nights at a pet-friendly place there for tonight and tomorrow night. Then we woke up this morning and realized that this was probably not such a good idea, either. I'd been told earlier that we needed to cancel our reservations by Sunday, though, or we'd lose the money. Soooo…

The thought occurred to me that maybe I could call homeless shelters in Lincoln City – maybe they knew someone who could use a warm room for two nights. So I called a couple places – one wasn't open, yet, another one told me that because of the virus they'd already found a hotel to put their homeless people in. She thanked me, though, for wanting to do this, and seemed really grateful for my gesture.

When I realized I wasn't going to be able to use this room to help homeless folks, I called Sailor Jack's to cancel our reservation. And Angie at the desk said we hadn't been charged, yet, and we wouldn't be! She cancelled our reservations without charge! AND told us to stay safe up here. I told her we'd be coming down again later and we'd be seeing her.

I'm just… I'm kind of teary-eyed here. People are so kind. I'm seeing the best in folks right now.

If you have a clear sky tonight go outside and take a gander at the stars. From our home, Venus looks HUGE tonight. The frogs are just starting to make their music. There's peace and beauty all around us.

The stars help put everything in perspective for me. The universe is so much bigger than our problems – and I find that oddly reassuring. I always say hi to Mom when I look at the stars. And now I say hi to Dad, too.

Solace at the Cemetary

In these panicked times
In these fretful, frenzied, frantic times
I have found solace at the cemetery.
The shells of those who've lived
here and moved on
to whatever comes beyond
no longer need to distance themselves
from anyone, from me.
I find peace with them – the chrysalises
of my friends – Mike, Rachael, and Debby.

I wander amid the tombstones, snapping
photos of them, and the spinning wheels –
the bright spinners are the only movement
in the cemetery and I feel
drawn to the movement of their rainbow
spinning, faster and faster as I approach,
in a show just for me.

I'm allowed to be here. In the sunshine.
In the peace of the cemetery.
And no one disturbs me as I wander
through the final beds
for the shells of those who
are no longer scared of what lies ahead.
– Karen Molenaar Terrell

March 18, 2020

Son is traveling through Germany right now. Borders are closing. Restaurants and shops are closing. Travel is restricted. Tourists are restricted from certain cities. Things are getting a little complicated for travelers - and not just those traveling in Germany. I know my son isn't the only one out there, trying to negotiate a rapidly shifting landscape. I send out a request to my FB friends on every continent - let's be aware of the "strangers within our borders" - and reach out to help each other, when we can.

We need a support group for Parents of Adventurous Children. PAC. I understand better what my mom must have gone through as she raised my brothers and me. I am learning a lot of Mom lessons, for sure.

Update: After riding eight trains today, Andrew made it into de Nederlands. He'll be staying at the BioArt Laboratories in Eindhoven. He writes: "This is gonna be a very different experience, I'm so excited. I think it's gonna be time to buckle down on some art and weirdness."

March 22, 2020

Here's a Dad-lesson for the times: I once asked Dad what he was feeling as he careened down that slope on K2, headed for the drop over the cliff and certain death. Was he scared?

No, he said, it was exhilarating! He was totally in the moment. Enjoying the ride. He knew everything was going to go black for him soon – and knew there was nothing he could do about that – so he just settled into the moment and enjoyed it.

And when I've thought about his answer, I've realized I can relate to it. The times I've been most scared – most filled with unspeakable dread – are the times when I've focused on the future – on all the many scary things that MIGHT happen – rather than what was actually happening with me right now – in this moment.

When I've found myself – in the moment – facing a challenge – it's not been scary, really. I've focused on the problem at hand and dealt with it.

Rock-climbing is all about the moment – I remember a piton clinking down a rock cliff when I was mid-way up a climb once – I remember looking up to the man belaying me and I remember him looking down at me – I remember that exchange of looks – I remember how quickly I faced the moment and hauled myself up that rock face. There was no time for fear. It was very cool, actually.

I remember feeling that same in-the-momentness when I gave birth to Xander. I'd been told, suddenly, that there were

complications in the delivery and I was going to need a
caesarean section. I remember being wheeled down to the
operating room and Mom's face looking at me from the foot of
the gurney. I asked her to call a friend (a Christian Science
practitioner) to pray and she hurried off to do that.

And, in that moment, as things were happening, I didn't feel
any fear at all. I felt this amazing sense of peace envelope me. I
was totally focused on the moment. I could feel the love from
all the doctors and nurses – wanting only the best for me and
my child – I could feel the love from Scotty and my parents,
and my midwife. Everything was happening very quickly, but I
felt strangely calm – I wasn't afraid about what MIGHT
happen, IF… I was living in that moment.

When I got down to the OR, they hooked me up to all these
machines. I remember the eyes of the medical staff looking at
the machines, then back to me, and I could see they were
puzzled – and then suddenly they were all telling me to push! –
like they were fans at a football game, rooting me on! And they
were celebrating with me!

My baby was born the old-fashioned way that day. (But it
wouldn't have mattered, really, if he'd entered the world in
another manner – the form of the birth wasn't important to me.)
One of the surgical nurses was actually crying! She said she'd
never been able to witness a vaginal birth before – and it was
really beautiful.

Later I learned what the CS practitioner had told my mom that
morning: "Life loves that baby!"

And I know this, for sure, Life loves ALL of us – each and every one of Her children – it doesn't matter where we are or what we're doing or what the time – it doesn't matter if we're on a rock cliff or on an operating table, or in quarantine or on the Moon – Love is there with us, loving us, eternally and always.

Let's do what we need to do for each other right now, humanly. Physical distance, but not isolation – knowing that we are the very expressions of Love, loved by Love, never separated or isolated from Love. Living in this moment.

March 25, 2020

I went for a drive – Scott had the television news on and I felt the need to go into my mental "closet" and bring my thoughts close to the presence of Love. I pulled over to watch Mount Baker turn pink in the setting sun and a song from the *Christian Science Hymnal* came to me – "O Gentle Presence" (with words by Mary Baker Eddy). I sang the hymn to Mount Baker and felt the comforting words wrap around me.

This line from "O Gentle Presence" especially resonates with me right now – "O Life divine, that owns each waiting hour" – I mean…think about that! God – Life, Truth, and Love – owns, manages, and governs EVERY hour – even the "waiting" ones. There is never a moment outside of Love's control – never a moment not created by God. Those moments when we're waiting to learn our loved ones are safe; when we're waiting to hear the prognosis; when we're waiting for the plane to land; or the tests to come back; or the quarantine to be lifted – God owns even THOSE moments. Whoah.

March 27, 2020

I've been cleaning out cupboards and going through old boxes-trying to get rid of some of the stuff we've collected over the years. I ran upstairs to do something and when I came down I found this "USA Weekend" magazine on the dining room floor. I looked at the cover and had this moment of ...what?! Weekend getaways?! Invitation etiquette?! What world is "USA Weekend" living in?! And then I realized this was from 2004 - probably fell out of one of the boxes. It made me feel a little nostalgic for a time when whether or not Pete Rose got in the Hall of Fame was the biggest concern some people had.

Update: Andrew made it through US Customs in Chicago. I was able to track his flight from Amsterdam. And now I'm tracking his flight to Seattle!

Cleaning During a Time of Quarantine

The cleaning started with the bedroom – I vacuumed, dusted,
filled five bags full of clothes to take to the thrift shop
when it opens again someday, and washed the curtains
so they glowed golden in the sunshine from bottom to top.

Next it was the cupboard in the family room – sorting
electronics, gizmos and gadgets, a springy door stop,
a weird stretchy thing for exercising, the sons' old toys,
and treasure! – an old card with love from Moz and Pop.

Then the closet under the stairs – a file full of paperwork
that was important once, costumes, Thomas the Tank Engine
train set, baskets full of old magazines, and board games,
an old slide projector and carousel, winter clothing in bins.

And today I awoke slowly from a lovely afternoon nap
to see curtains glowing golden in the afternoon sunlight.
Who could have guessed to find such beauty and peace
in clean light-filled curtains – in that simple sight?
– Karen Molenaar Terrell

March 31, 2020

The sons are safe and I am a happy mama.

We're Going to Let Dad's Celebration "Season" a Little

Karen writes: *Tom Vogl, from the Mountaineers, and I have been emailing back and forth the last week about the memorial celebration The Mountaineers had planned to host for Dad on April 12th in Seattle. I expressed concern to Tom that it might be hard for people to fly into Seattle in April what with the current situation with the coronavirus - Tom had been thinking the same thing. It has been decided to cancel the celebration in April and reschedule for a later time. We wanted to let everyone know now so they can still get refunds on their flights.*

Tom Vogl writes: *While I am disappointed we won't have the opportunity to gather in celebration of Dee's life next month, I think it's the right decision for the health and well-being of our community. Stay tuned for information about Plan B. I'll work with Karen on a new date - possibly this summer or next fall.*

Karen writes: *As Tom Hornbein says - we're going to let Dad's celebration "season" a little.*

Cari Hornbein writes: *I just got back from visiting Dad. Was looking forward to seeing him again in April, but a wise choice to postpone!*

We'll See How This Goes

Four years ago, during the last election season, strangers would suddenly appear and comment on my public posts and they would say things with weird phrasing and syntax - stuff like "you are a big banana butt" and "you are a person brainless" - and sometimes their names were spelled with characters that are not used in the English language (μονοσε πουλι). These strangers would tell me to eff off and wished harm to me and my friends. It was an odd and interesting time.

I blocked those people (to block the names with weird characters I had to do a copy and paste - my keyboard doesn't include weird characters on it) and learned from that experience to disallow commenting on my public posts from people who aren't my friends.

I'm pretty sure now - looking back - that these strangers were not fellow citizens of my country. (Duh, right?) I'm not even sure that they were actually human beings.

I don't want my posts to be divisive - that is not my intent here. I don't want to see my friends ganging up on each other and calling each other names. I don't want to promote hate here. I don't want to let myself or my posts be manipulated or used to create havoc and confusion.

But...

I also have a real need to share things that matter to me; to share things that are important to me; to share the things that give me hope, and the things that feel like a punch in the gut, too; and to share things that might help us learn from each other.

I am struggling with how to proceed on FB. Honestly, sometimes the hate and mean-ness I encounter here is so overwhelming that I feel the need to leave. And sometimes I just get bored with myself - yada yada blah blah blah - and realize I have nothing more to add.

Anyway. We'll see how this goes...

Jeff Chase writes: *I think it's good to take a break sometimes from social media - even if my 66 friends (including several deceased) mostly ignore me. We all need to recharge. But if you ever think you're not making a difference, please let that go. You have enriched my life more than I could ever tell you. Thank you.*

Karen writes: *Oh Jeff! Thank YOU! I'm so glad to know you, "little bro."*

Steve D. writes: *Sounds like bot accounts to me. I've only been checking in with FB every couple days because it's full of crazy people now.*

Karen writes: *I know, right? And... I'm ascared I might be one of 'em.*

Steve D. writes: *Nah. Of all the crazy folk I know you're among the most sane. Or we're nuts and everyone else is sane. Seriously though, FB has gotten hostile.*

Jolyne writes: *In their defense, you kind of are a banana butt.*

Karen writes: *Jolyne, you have given me my first laugh out loud of the day! Thank you! I really needed that.*

Peravena writes: *Your words are golden. As I discovered 50 plus years ago.*

Karen writes: *I'm blessed to have had you for my fifth grade teacher, Peravena! You nurtured your students' talents; you helped me see myself as a writer. I'm so glad we've been able to reconnect here.*

Diane L. writes: *I understand your struggle and it gets overwhelming sometimes to see the negativity, but I hope you don't stop posting. Your posts are thoughtful and genuine. I appreciate and need them.*

Karen writes: *Thank you so much, Diane! Your kind words mean a lot to me. I'm so glad FB connected us!*

Karen Troianello writes: *The goodness you share, the thoughtful heartfelt opinions, the joy you exude - not to mention your fine photographic eye, are some of the good things on this platform.*

Karen Rippberger writes: *The world needs more real Karens. Please stay. You are a light in a dark sky. You've taught and consoled and uplifted and unknowingly reprimanded me when I've needed it. It is a wonderful gift.*

Karen writes: *Thank you for your encouraging words, Karens! You both rock!*

April

THE WORLDWIDE OUTBREAK of the coronavirus currently exceeds 1.3 million confirmed cases across more than 150 countries. The virus originated in central China in late 2019, and its spread has crippled the travel and event industries. There are now confirmed coronavirus cases across all 50 states in the United States. A ban on most travel from continental Europe (including the United Kingdom and Ireland) began March 13, 2020, at midnight, but does not apply to American citizens or permanent legal residents. Additionally, the Department of State announced a Global Level 4 Health Advisory on March 19, 2020, advising U.S. citizens to avoid all international travel and for U.S. citizens currently abroad to return home if flights are still available.

-Watson, Zach. Shields. "CDC Cronavirus Travel Updates: What to Know About Current Travel Restrictions.". US News and World Report, 7 April, 2020 (https://travel.usnews.com/features/should-i-travel-what-you-need-to-know-about-coronavirus-and-traveling)

Today Is Thursday

Today is Thursday. Just in case any of you were wondering.

Alrighty. Carry on then...

Elizabeth E. Fisher writes*: Did you say you were thirsty?*

April 2, 2020

How we all doing? If you'd like to pop in and share some piece of good news, it would be most appreciated.

Rhonda M. writes*: I spent the day cutting back blackberries. Looking forward to September. What a wonderful day to be outside watching the eagles and enjoying the sun with Dave.*

Cathleen M. writes*: Weather forecast for the coming week is looking good.*

Stephani Z. writes*: My kid is painting!*

Heidi L. writes*: Rain is coming down. Puppy is snoring. Fire is roaring. Relaxing.*

Laura R. writes*: My niece Danika and the students and other teachers of the Travelling School had been marooned/quarantined in Peru for a couple weeks. They all made it back to the States last Saturday.*

Elly H. writes*: Kids doing tele-school, daughter is doing tele-mental health counseling, son-in-law doing government stuff, the elderly here are doing tele-financial counseling, and I am mask-making. Feeling okay.*

Mary Ann writes*: I am thrilled. I got to see my grandboys today..Yes, we practiced social distancing and were outside - a short visit, but wonderful!!!*

Andrea B. writes*: After a couple of days of fear and planning as though my husband and I would live only a few more* *months, I finally seem to have gotten my head back on straight. An online pastel painting class has helped a great deal! Here is an abstract sunset I did a couple of days ago. (And thank you for asking.)*

James A. writes: *I think I'm over-eating on home-baked cookies!*

Mary M. writes: *The West Seattle turkey *finally* put in an appearance for Scott this evening!*

Edward V. writes: *Had a good family Zoom meeting today.*

Pam A. writes: *Edward, we might be doing that tonight with in-laws and my daughter had a FaceTime dinner with my husband and I for his birthday last week*

Leanne M. writes: *I did my first online grocery order at Fred Meyer. Couldn't get a "pickup" date in Burlington, but got one today at FM store on Lakeway in Bellingham. It was so easy!!*

Diane L writes: *I found everything I needed in the house to make masks for our hospital.*

Pam A. writes: *I heard that the first two positive Coranavirus victims from our area, that I know, are recovered now. Also, my run today felt great and I'm so thankful for healthy lungs.*

Janice M. writes: *Skye and I are getting lots of jogs, walks and gardening time together. She is loving retrieving balls, chasing dead leaves in the breezes, and romping up and down the halls. She is unaware of the virus.*

Peg S. writes: *My neighbors brought us homemade cookies today and these great thank you cards for a little something we did for them. It was so nice!*

David Molenaar writes: *Went for a 21-mile ride tonight after work and saw a magnificent sunset.*

Estevan V. writes: *My wife and I are expecting our first child in the next day or so.*

Karen writes: *That makes me so happy!!! And gives me hope for our world!*

Susan R. writes: *Hi Karen, I have a loaf of bread in the oven. Yum! Can't wait to have a slice - I need a snack. While I wait for that I'm watching "The Great Food Truck Race."*

Eileen A. writes: *Our adult kids are back from Thailand. 14 day-quarantine from their jobs, but so happy they are back safe. Everyone in Asia wears masks (mostly from respect to others), so they did, too. I am going to wear one when I go grocery shopping next week. Made myself a Japanese mask from a YouTube video.*

Leanne M. writes: *Bow Hill Blueberry is open. They have a side window, with a shield, for you to make your purchases.*

Karen writes: *Yes! I bought a bag of heirloom berries there for pie!*

Elizabeth E. Fisher writes: *I made Shepherd's Pie tonight and it was soooo good!*

Theresa B. writes: *I am working at home and having a glass of wine. I got a call from a friend in New Zealand and she is* *unable to leave, but says it is like being quarantined in Paradise. Frankincat got out, but was nabbed by a herd dog and herded back in. People are suffering and afraid, but I get to call them and provide some comfort. I am profoundly grateful.*

Kathie B. writes*: My homeschooling efforts are going well and my husband retires the end of May.*

Mary B. writes*: Paul's daughter, Angie is having a baby in July. We are so happy!*

Karen writes*: That's AWESOME news.*

Debra M. writes*: Kids are happy - they played with cousins online, did their schoolwork, came out of their rooms for a bit! I painted more rocks for my Easter Rock Hunt project and made a video with art palette tips to share with an art course I am taking; potatoes are growing great in the yard....and weather is great! Rain, sunshine, cool breezes. Grateful for so much! And for you, too.*

Karen writes*: And I am grateful for YOU!*

Nicole B. writes*: It was a beautiful day. We started a new garden. That is enough to make anyone happy.*

Taraleen writes*: We are taking the time to make and eat delicious, healthy food! I'm coloring, playing games, taking walks and doing yoga. I'm learning to be more still which is really hard for me; I tend to stay pretty busy in order to avoid feeling sometimes. But this experience is all about learning and relearning. Letting go. Recognizing we have no control and accepting that. Love you Karen.*

Karen writes: *I love you, too!*

Pam B. writes: *Here is a photo of a beautiful bouquet that a friend of mine just picked. I love all the positive news in this comment thread. Thank you so much to everyone for sharing!!*

Ricky F. writes: *A little black feral cat I've been feeding has finally decided to trust me enough so that she comes to me for affection as well as food.*

Karen writes: *Ricky, our once-feral cat is now exposing his belly for rubs.*

Liz P. writes: *My anise bush is blooming dark pink and beautiful, along with all the millions of other flowers in my yard, mostly "weeds."*

Michelle D. writes: *I'm meeting my co-interns tonight over Zoom!! These are the peeps I'll be spending 80hrs/week with!!*

Dawn B. writes: *Next week is going to be sunny and beautiful and your heart will soar with the birds. When I get sad, first thing I do is look for the low clouds. Sure enough they are low enough to get into my heart, so I know it is just temporary and will pass.*

Victoria Y. writes: *Edward and his wife had a beautiful baby girl and Nigel got home from his mission in Chile!!*

Karen writes: *Wonderful news!*

Danny O. writes: *If the protagonist in an autobiography is hanging off the cliff, not to worry. He's got to live to write the book.*

Karen Troianello writes: *I fell down in the garden (tripping over my own feet) but got back up hardly worse for the wear. Well, a little worse. But I managed to say to my mom as I was falling, "I'm ok, I am falling - but I am ok - that crash was just me hitting the house - I am ok."*

Karen writes: *I'm so glad you're ok!*

Jackie C. writes: *Me and Hubby still together and in love after all these years (not always easy, but never is!), kids doing GREAT. Both in DE, Russell graduates this year. Both have (had) jobs until coronavirus. Jess is a Jr. and has a bf and he asked her to prom so we had a mom/daughter prom dress shop date recently. I still have the job of my dreams, although that's a real rough ride right now...but that's ok, cuz I'm still there fightin' the good fight....we are all healthy. Dad just left, he visited for a month and turned 80 while he was here (so terribly sorry about your dad, Karen). Russell just turned 18. Hubby and I both still have our jobs and are considered essential employees. How's that for some stuff to be grateful for?! Love u girl.*

Karen writes: *I love you, too!*

Claudia B. writes: *My daughter and I are making masks for the family - but since we have such a large family that may take a while...*

Janet D. writes: *I got to hug my girl today! So happy my two are safe!*

William W. writes: *Got my degree today!*

Virginia K. writes: Dennis and I have been married for 22 years tomorrow and we made masks.

Wanda K. writes: My daughter and grandson brought us groceries today, after she and my son-in-law braved the long lines to do the shopping - not just for themselves and us, but also for a neighbor of theirs who can't do his own shopping!

Sheryl D. writes: The sun was out and I got to work in my yard...

Joyce N. writes: My hyacinths are blooming

Jeff Chase writes: It's Friday. Thank you, Lord. I made it to the weekend!!

Beth W. writes: Baked this cake yesterday.

Cari Hornbein writes: I just picked up my Fred Meyer order -- no organic romaine, bleach, or paper towels, but at least I got the wine and cheese!

Pamm F. writes: Dave and I are both working from home and are still receiving paychecks.

Katrina S. writes: Brownies. And great results on my electronics project.

Peter Molenaar writes: Atmospheric CO2 concentrations are rising more slowly.

Lisa K. writes: I got me some baby chickens.

Theresa B. writes: I baked a raspberry blackberry pie.

Diana P. writes: *I shaved my husband's head, so now the back of his head looks like a checkerboard.....by accident.*

Brynn Z writes: *I found my favorite pen so now I can write again*

Marc Z. writes: *My dog, Allie Babba, has created a load of saw dust for the garden, having become queen destroyer of sticks.*

Jim S. writes: *Four new baby turtles today!*

James A.writes: *New Zealand is seeing a decline in new cases after just two weeks!*

Pamm F. writes: *We are planning our Easter dinner zoom with the kids & grandbabies. You can't always get what ya want, but ya get what ya need.*

Karen writes: *Mowed and pruned the Secret Garden and planted wildflower seeds. Bike ride in the sunshine. It's gorgeous out there!*

Laurie B. writes: *Went to Safeway and a very nice lady loaded all my ordered items into the car for me. She said that the tip I left for her would be put into the donation basket so folks who couldn't afford food could get some. Wow! I am really liking how folks are...*

Karen writes: *Took the dog for a walk and saw honeybees going in and out of the cedar tree again - I hadn't seen them there for a while and was concerned about them.*

Wendy A. writes: *Yes, they were swarming my Lapin cherry yesterday, too. A sight for sore eyes!*

Laurie B. writes: *Loads of honeybees today in the garden. Little legs packed full of pollen.*

Deb C. writes: *15.5 mile bike ride today in the fresh air. Felt great.*

George S. writes: *This morning's before-dawn call and response from a pair of mockingbirds. I've had the time for longer phone chats with friends; flowers are in blooming profusion. The waning moon smiles on the earth, kale and chard from the garden, and the first tomato plants in the ground.*

Jessie N. writes: *I dug out my summer clothes, and my shorts still fit!! It's the little things.*

Cheryl G. writes: *Doing great! The weather is good, the garden is ready for the seeds and plants I have. My son came home to help us and is here for a while. My family is well.*

Also, in the midst of this terrible virus, good has come. We have been reminded of the things that truly matter and we have slowed down. Happy Easter, Karen.

Karen writes: *Happy Easter, Cheryl!*

Tami W. writes: *Run, walk, bike, gardening!!!*

Kathleen W. writes: *Just got an announcement that Niece and Nephew's first little baby is on the way. Due in November. Growing Family. I love being an auntie.*

Diane L. writes: *Delightful socially-distanced walk yesterday, bluebird sky, Cascades white with snow...we could even see Mt. Hood. And the trees are beginning to burst into bloom.*

Jenny S. writes: *I am almost done with cleaning out our garage and sorting thru three tubs of old photographs. Threw most of them away and now down to one shoe box of sorted photos and several envelopes to mail to others.*

Janet D. writes: *Gave a dog a belly rub by Blue River yesterday.*

Joe T. writes: *Saw a gold finch at my feeder today!*

Pamm F. writes: *Read a bedtime story to my granddaughter on Facetime.*

Elizabeth E. Fisher writes: *I have spent the last three days making fabric masks for my kids and grandkids. More mandates to wear fabric masks on the horizon. I am actually having fun.*

Karen writes: *I now have SIX bags of clothes and two boxes full of stuff to take to Value Village, and the recycle bin is filled to the brim with shredded junkmail and old documents I haven't needed for maybe a decade - with another big box full of MORE detritus sitting next to it. Cupboard downstairs is organized; closet under the stairs is looking good; bedroom is shiny and clean; and I can actually walk into my office and know where to find things now. Next: Dad's old desk.*

Working on some writing projects.

Watched "Bridesmaids" last night - I so love Melissa McCarthy in that one!

And I believe it is time to make another pie.

Andrew: You want to meditate with me?
Karen: Yeah. I'd like that.

April 3, 2020

I made one of those no pleat masks to go shopping this morning. I posted a picture of it. One of my FB friends told me I needed to get my rear end home. So then I felt guilty for grocery-shopping - and I took the picture down. These times are making me more neurotic than I already was.

(There were more people wearing masks than weren't in the store.)

April 6, 2020

No one "deserves" to be sick.

When I took my first trip to Europe in 1980 I was fascinated by the old buildings. Some of them were, like, 700 years old! (Where I live the oldest buildings are maybe 150 years old.) I remember wanting to get up next to them and touch them – feel the vibes of all the people who touched them before me in history.

While he was giving me a tour of historic old buildings, my Dutch friend told me that during The Black Plague the entries to villages were actually designed to keep the sick people out – the sick were left to wander without food or shelter or succor in-between the towns. They were left on their own, alone and shunned.

I remember thinking how grateful I was that our world had become more civilized since then.

Right after I got back from Europe the AIDS epidemic hit, and I saw that we maybe hadn't become all that more civilized. I saw people being shunned again. Some preachers told their congregations that these people deserved to be sick, and deserved to die.

It was a terrible time.

And now we have this. I'm seeing a lot that is giving me hope for our world – I'm seeing people coming together in a way

I've never witnessed to help each other. And I'm seeing some things, too, that make me realize we still have a ways to go.

NObody "deserves" to be sick. NObody "deserves" to die. No matter your politics or religion, your age or medical history, or errors in judgment – no one "deserves" sickness and death.

In reality, we are all God's innocent children. There is no guilt attached to us – to any of us. Every moment we are fresh and new and uncontaminated. There is no disease that is more powerful than God's love and grace.

You are Love's precious child.

To answer any questions folks might be having about how Christian Science churches are responding to government restrictions during this time of sheltering-in-place, I thought it might be helpful to bring in the words of the founder of Christian Science, Mary Baker Eddy: "Whatever changes come to this century or to any epoch, we may safely submit to the providence of God, to common justice, to the maintenance of individual rights, and to governmental usages…When Jesus was questioned concerning obedience to human law, he replied: 'Render to Caesar the things that are Caesar's,' even while you 'render to God the things that are God's.'"

"I believe in obeying the laws of the land."
– Mary Baker Eddy, Miscellany (p 220)

Resting in the Arms of Love

I went to bed fretting and frightened
imagining all kinds of doom
I read a little to settle my thoughts
and finally closed my eyes and slept

I awoke in the dark quiet early hours
surrounded by an all-knowing, loving
presence bigger than the sky – assuring
me of endless, eternal, infinite good

I started to get up – wanting to share this
moment with my FB friends – but then I
stopped, holding on to that moment for
myself, resting in Love a little longer
– Karen Molenaar Terrell

Quiet Time of Quarantine

Enfolded in a sense of perfect well-being
a pure peace and stillness and quiet
surrounds me as I glide on my bike past
green fields and red barns and little yellow
flowers framing the craggly snow-topped
volcano in the background. I can smell
the briny bay and the sweet new buds
on the alders and the earthy scent of the
dairy farm – familiar and comforting.
One or two cars pass me, but I am mostly
alone on this road on the flats. Is it selfish
to say that this quiet time of quarantine
has been a blessing for me? I have thirsted
for a break from the angst and agitation,
the buzzing busyness and frantic, frenetic
frightful panicked pace of politics and ego.
I am enjoying this simple time of just be-ing.
– Karen Molenaar Terrell

April 20, 2020

A couple of you have messaged me to let me know how much you've missed my "drives with Dad." I really appreciate your kind words and thoughtfulness, and taking the time to write me. I miss my drives with Dad, too - I miss his spontaneous geology lectures; I miss looking for Mount Baker with him; I miss talking about the mountains we climbed together and remembering our adventures; I miss his keen observations; I miss his courage in the face of pain and adversity. He inspired me. He continues to inspire me.

Dad was born during the flu epidemic of 1918 and died on January 19th - just two days before the first coronavirus case was reported in Washington State. I'm so grateful we never had to be separated from each other because of the virus. I'm not sure he would have understood.

Essential Travel

From my place of privilege in the spring green farmland – a place made for long, quiet solo bike rides that begin right outside my doorstep – a place where self-isolating has become a time of sweet retirement for me – is it my role to judge what is "essential travel" for that young mother enclosed in a small apartment with rambunctious toddlers from morning until night? Maybe that drive through the countryside with her little ones IS essential to her well-being. Maybe the woman in the grips of a dark debilitating depression desperately needs to leave her home and go for a drive so she can see children laughing in front yards and folks mowing their lawns, and be assured that life is still being lived. Maybe that person we see driving on the roads hasn't been to the supermarket for two weeks and needs to get groceries for another two. I can't know what goes on in everyone else's life. I can only make sure that I make the best choices I can make in my own life – choices that come from a place of Love.
– Karen Molenaar Terrell

April 22, 2020

During this time of self-isolating, my solo bike rides through the countryside around my home have helped keep me sane. Birdsong and budding trees and the air alive with bees and butterflies – these are the things that refresh and invigorate me. Happy Earth Day!

What a lovely day. Played cribbage and Stratego with Andrew. (He would have beaten me at Stratego - I was down to a handful of guys who could actually move - but he'd lost all his guys who could detonate bombs and my flag was surrounded by bombs - so we agreed to disarmament and called it done.) Andrew showed me a new card trick and I was laughing so hard I had tears, literally, streaming down my face. (Being isolated with Drew and Scott is the best! It's like being quarantined with a couple of comedy stars.)

After board games, I pulled out the umbrella and went for a walk with Sam the Wonder Dog (I love the sound of rain pattering on a bumbershoot - there's something about that sound that's really soothing for me). Came home and put together a bumbleberry pie and while that was baking I sat down to watch "Roman Holiday" - I don't remember ever watching that movie before - it was the perfect movie for a rainy afternoon.

And now I think I'll get a fire going in the woodstove and maybe read a good book.

Hope you all are doing well out there.

Love from Bow.

79

Andrew: You want to meditate?
Karen: Yeah. Yeah, I do

Dean Wrzeszcz, October 11, 1957 to April 4, 2020

My friend. Dean Wrzeszcz, died of COVID today. Dean is the man who christened me "Wingoov Vowel Hoarder." You have only to look at his last name to understand.

Dean, I'm so very glad I got to know you while you were here! You've made a difference in my life. You've made a difference to the world.

Dean (aka "Nietz") writes (in 2008): *Hello, Karen! I worked until 3 a.m., so I thought I'd check in early this April 1st. I love you. (I'm saying that 'cause I'm loopy tired, but it doesn't mean I'm not sincere.)*

May I have a slice of haggis and a pint, please? And, what the hell, a shot of tequila just for fun! And let me know when the comfy chair's available. I don't believe I've ever had the pleasure!

Karen writes: *My dearest Nietz (and you really are my dearest Nietz. I mean, I don't actually know any other Nietzes, but still...).*

I love you, too, my wise and witty friend. And here's your pint and your haggis (good luck with that) and your shot to wash it all down.

And you've never had a turn in the comfy chair...?!! We'll have to see what we can arrange...

Your sister in neuroticity,
Karen.

May

SAVANNAH, Ga. (AP) — Georgia authorities arrested a white father and son Thursday and charged them with murder in the February shooting death of a black man they had pursued in a truck after spotting him running in their neighborhood.

The charges came more than two months after Ahmaud Arbery, 25, was killed on a residential street just outside the port city of Brunswick. National outrage over the case swelled this week after cellphone video that appeared to show the shooting.

Those close to Arbery celebrated the news but also expressed frustration at the long wait.

"This should have occurred the day it happened," said Akeem Baker, one of Arbery's close friends in Brunswick. "There's no way without the video this would have occurred. I'm just glad the light's shining very bright on this situation."

Bynam, Russ. Nadler, Ben. "Father, Son, Charged with Killing Black Man Ahmaud Arbery." AP News, 7 May, 2020. (https://apnews.com/article/96990a5023927df289c934d2decd9 0b8)

Sometimes I Just Need Happy Endings

I am watching one of those movies where music plays in the background the whole time, and I know the big problem is going to be solved by the end, and everyone will be friends. I'm embarrassed I'm watching this. But sometimes I just need happy endings.

Alrighty. Carry on then...

May 1, 2020

From a side conversation with another "Karen":

I was actually named "Nancy Jo" for three days. Then my dad took an office poll and "Karen" won. Yeah. I was named by Dad's colleagues. Considering that they were a bunch of geologists, I guess I could have done worse than be named "Karen." I might have been named "Sedimentary" or "Igneous" or "Schist" or "Cretaceous." I never actually felt like a "Karen" until it became a comic meme. Now I love to tell people my name. With a straight face. My name is a great one-liner.

May 2, 2020

Taking the dog for a walk. I round the corner and see my neighbor (and former student) across the road. "Hi Michael!" I holler. He looks over and smiles and waves. "Am I a fashion plate?" I ask him. I am wearing floral-patterned garden shoes, purple knee-high socks, baggy denim capri pants two sizes too big and covered in mud at the knees from gardening, my standard black t-shirt and a black fleece jacket. Michael grins at the picture I make. "I just don't care anymore," I tell him, laughing.

Michael joins me in the laugh and points to his beard. "You see my beard?" he asks. "I don't care anymore, either."

We laugh for a moment with each other, and then wish one another a good night.

Priorities have shifted.

I am responsible about wearing a face mask when I'm among other people - I know this is something I can do to help others. But to offer another perspective on face masks - I am hard of hearing and, for me, face masks bring some real frustrations. Peoples' voices are muffled and I can't hear well what they're saying. Their lips are covered so I can't read their lips. And the mask's straps get tangled in my hearing aids and pull them off or make them beep - so I often don't wear my hearing aids with the mask. And the social cues that I depend on - seeing a person's smile or frown - are hampered by the mask. In my years of solitary walks, I've also come to depend on a smile as a safety tool - I smile at other people to let them know that I'm not a threat, and that I don't see THEM as a threat, either. Smiles have been huge for me and have gotten me through some sketchy situations.

May 3, 2020

Karen: Is it Sunday now?
Andrew: I suspect it is.

May 19, 2020

I'm guessing that pretty much all politicians – including the ones we like – have found a way to politicize this current challenge. And I don't blame or judge any of them for doing it – that's what politicians do. But I think we need to be aware of it – and I think we need to each be honest with ourselves about our own biases, too. Wouldn't it be great if people just wanted to do right by each other – without concern about political parties and agendas?

I've Been Looking at Polls

I've been looking at polls
looking at graphs
trying to determine
if our world's going to last.
This poll says this
and this graph says that.
Does it look like the curve
is starting to go flat?
And which of our leaders
is gaining support?
What type of leader?
What flavor? What sort?

I guess I could spend a lot
of time looking at graphs –
looking for hope there
looking for laughs.
But maybe instead I should
go right to the Source –
go to Life, Love, and Truth
and feel the Force.
Everything can change
in a moment, you see.
But I don't need a poll
to know Love is the key.
– Karen Molenaar Terrell

What I Miss

I most miss open smiles and hugs full of love.
I miss the waitress at the Colophon Cafe who takes
my order for African peanut soup as the music
of friends chatting and laughing at the other
tables washes over us, and bathes us in their joy.
I miss stopping to chat on the boardwalk and
meeting old friends, and new. I miss getting
to know people as we wait in line at the store,
and running into former students in the aisles.
I miss buying mochas for the stranger standing
on the corner. I miss the buskers and their music,
and the color and energy of the Farmers Market.

Here's what I will miss when this is over –
I'll miss the quiet roads and clean blue skies.
I'll miss the No Car Days and the time at home
with family. I'll miss the weeks without a schedule
and losing track of time. I'll miss the stillness
and peace and time to reflect. I'll miss this time
alone. I'll miss the uninterrupted time to create
and garden and sing and think. I'll miss the time
to catch up with correspondence, and the time
to sort and recycle the flotsam and jetsam that
washes from the mailbox and onto our kitchen
counter Monday through Saturday.

I'm going to remember to be grateful for what
I had then, and grateful for what I have now,
and grateful for what I'll have tomorrow, too.
– Karen Molenaar Terrell

May 20, 2020

We have just a tiny scrap of existence here
– a miniscule piece of our eternity –
to love and learn and live
and leave something good behind.
Let's not waste it on nothings.
– Karen Molenaar Terrell

As I was scrolling through Facebook I saw a post by a friend,
sharing that she'd just lost her mother. Her mother had gone
into the hospital on a Wednesday and was dead on Sunday. Her
death was a surprise to everyone. As I looked through my
friend's pictures of her mom, I realized that her mom was
probably about my age. That realization brought me up short.
Whoah. And then I thought of the loved ones I've lost in the
last several years – some of them my age, and some of them
younger – and it gave me pause.

I am not afraid of death. I'm maybe afraid of the pain involved
in death, but I'm not afraid of death itself. If, as I believe, my
consciousness will continue on and continue to learn and
unfold – that would be fine. And if death is really the end – that
would be fine, too – I mean, I won't be around to feel one way
or the other about it, right? No, I'm not afraid of death – but I
hope that what I do here, during my time here, will make a
difference for the people who come after me. I hope my time
here will mean something, you know? I don't want to waste
even a minute of it on ridiculous rivalries, and empty quests for
fame and wealth. I don't want to waste my life on nothings.
Life is too short. We only have one shot at this.

The Humbling

Unfed, shred, and shed
every humbling shrinking
the ego until it loses all
hold, all importance, all
power and perspective
shifts and what's true
emerges from the tatters.
– Karen Molenaar Terrell

May 21, 2020

Andrew: You want to catch a sunset with me?!
Karen: Let's do it!

May 25, 2020

My new mask arrived and I was pretty excited to take it for a spin on the Bellingham boardwalk and see how it worked for me. As someone who is hard-of-hearing, masks can be kind of problematic for me: I can't read people's lips when they're wearing masks; people's voices are muffled through masks; I can't see the facial expressions that tell me if someone's friendly or hostile; I can't send my own smile out into the world to let people know I'm (mostly) harmless; and my hearing aids get all tangled up in the straps of my face masks and start beeping at me. So when my new "smiley face" mask arrived I was hoping that – even though it couldn't make me hear any better – at least it might let people know that I'm smiling at them…

And the new mask worked! People can actually tell when I'm smiling now! The smiley face matches up with my eye wrinkles and sends the signal that I'm friendly - and people wave! Yee haw! This is huge, my friends - HUGE!!!

May 27, 2020

Andrew and I went for a hike at Squires Lake today - we heard
the deepest frog call we have ever heard, and saw these
massive tadpoles swimming around in the lake. Bull frogs.

A Lesson from Cows

Enclosed in man's fences
ears numbered and tagged
their bodies may be owned
by humans (as some humans
might brag) –
but the fences and tags
can't heed the flow
of Soul, put boundaries
on Love. Still they know
Love, still they show
Love.
– Karen Molenaar Terrell

How Many Black Men Have to Die for Things to Change?

What's on your mind? Facebook asks.
And I look at the little box and wonder
how I can possibly put into words
what I'm feeling right now –
I'm not sure there are any words
big enough for my feelings.
Our world is in desperate need –
in desperate need of love,
of honesty and kindness and wisdom.
And my heart breaks for our world
and for all its creatures.
Love bless us all – each and every one.
– Karen Molenaar Terrell

How Do You Argue with Love?

You can't argue with Love.
There's nothing in Love to insult, offend or attack.
There's nothing in Love to be hurt or to hit back.
Love doesn't see skin color – not white or black.
Love fills all space – and that's a fact.
– Karen Molenaar Terrell

The Real Trickle Down

I doubt we'll ever see money, wealth, and riches
trickling down from the top to the bottom –
strangely, wealth always seems to get stuck at the top.
But there's other stuff that trickles down –
stuff I pray will stop. When a leader fans the fires
and gets the hatred burning, and uses fear and lies
– I feel a real yearning for a future that holds
wisdom, love, and understanding – a future with
a fountain of hope at the top – cascading joy
and peace, and creating a rainbow of beauty
on its way down to the base.
– Karen Molenaar Terrell

Bring in the Murder Hornets!

Aaaaaand...now we have murder hornets.

Two new specimens of Asian giant hornet have turned up in the Pacific Northwest, suggesting that the invasive species made it through the winter despite efforts last year to stamp out the menace to North America's honeybees.

A big, yellow-and-black insect found dead in a roadway near Custer, Wash., has been identified as the Asian giant hornet, or Vespa mandarinia, Sven Spichiger, an entomologist at the Washington State Department of Agriculture, announced May 29. It was "probably a queen," he said, from a brood in a 2019 nest and now ready to found a colony of her own.

Milius, Susan. "Asian Giant Murder Hornet Sightings." Science News, 29 May, 2020, https://www.sciencenews.org/article/asian-giant-murder-hornet-sightings-washington-canada

Just Another Day in America

I've been debating whether or not to share this - it's kind of embarrassing. I think my Republican friends will appreciate the humor in this, though, and I think my Democrat friends will get a good guffaw from it, too. Yea and verily, may rich and poor, conservative and liberal, White and Black, gay and straight and purple and pink polka-dotted and zebra-striped come together in unity at this time to laugh at another classic Karen Moment.

So I came upon a couple of motorcyclists at the store. Their jackets were festooned in badges. The woman had a badge for Canada - which... I love Canada. And I noticed the man had a badge for Obama - and I was thinking these are my people, right?

So, as they were leaving, I said to the man, "I love everything you've got going on with those badges."

And the man said, "Really? I wasn't so sure the people on the west coast would appreciate this one," and he pointed to the Obama badge.

I told him I loved that one, and he seemed really surprised and pleased by this. And then I looked closer and saw that the badge actually said, "Obama: The biggest bada$$ mistake America ever made."

And I said, "Oh. I voted for him."

And the man said, "Yeah." And his eyes above the mask gave me the sweetest smile - kind of disappointed and sad - but really sweet. And then he said - and this was genuine, "But you have a really good day, okay?"

And I wished him a really good day back.

And so it goes. Another day in America

Mary Ellen writes: *Haha, awesome!!!!*

Karen writes: *I thought you'd appreciate this one, Mary Ellen.*

Mary Ellen writes: *I am the fun Republican!*

Karen writes: *I love who you are, Mary Ellen.*

June

As demonstrations continue across the country to protest the death of George Floyd, a black man killed while in Minneapolis police custody, Americans see the protests both as a reaction to Floyd's death and an expression of frustration over longstanding issues. Most adults say tensions between black people and police and concerns about the treatment of black people in the U.S. – in addition to anger over Floyd's death – have contributed a great deal to the protests, according to a new Pew Research Center survey.

-Parker, Kim. Horowitz, Juliana Menasce. Anderson, Monica. "Amid Protests, Majorities Across Racial and Ethnic Groups Express Support for the Black Lives Matter Movement." Pew Research Center, 12 June, 2020. (https://www.pewsocialtrends.org/2020/06/12/amid-protests-majorities-across-racial-and-ethnic-groups-express-support-for-the-black-lives-matter-movement/)

I Spend a Good Chunk of My Day Clicking Stuff

So when there's an on/off button to click, and it says "off" - does that mean it's already off or does that mean I have to click it to turn it off? I spend a good chunk of my day clicking stuff and not really sure what I'm doing...

Alrighty...carry on then....

June 3, 2020

Missing Dad and Moz today, but so glad they're not here to see what's happening to our poor country.

I spent an hour today driving around to the places Dad and I used to go on our drives together – feeling the echo of his presence still there, talking to me.

While I was on my drive, I had a flashback of a time when a young Black man in a hoodie stopped to open the door for Dad, and I remember how Dad took the time to stop and thank him before he went into the building. It was a brief exchange – very quick – but the power of the brotherly love I felt being exchanged between Dad and the young man is still with me.

Thinking of Moz and imagining her shaking with indignation and anger at the injustice and racism we're seeing – just as she did when I was a little girl and we encountered a racist at the Sears store. The man had nodded his head towards a Black family and said they should be shopping in their own store. When Moz understood what he was saying she was furious – "They have as much right to be here as you or me!" she told him, trembling with rage. The man realized, then, who he was dealing with in Moz and got all red in the face and scurried away. That was a moment I will never forget – it had a huge impact on me. I remember feeling very proud to be Moz's daughter.

I remember how Moz and Dad celebrated the night Obama got elected – they were both so happy. Dad said he never thought he'd live long enough to see an African-American in the White

House – his whole face was lit up with pride in his country. Moz had tears in her eyes with the joy she felt that night.

I'm so grateful I was raised by these people – so grateful I was brought up to see beyond the color of someone's skin to what was in the heart of people. My parents gave me a kind of freedom with that.

Andrew: Do you want to meditate with me?
Karen: I could really use that. Thank you.

June 4, 2020

I'm so glad I could be a part of the Black Lives Matter rally
today. I ran into some of my favorite people: the Templetons,
Bailey, Summer, Pam A., and Charles Atkinson. I cried (The
"Hands up! Don't shoot!" chant especially got to me). I
laughed (when one guy gave us the finger – I pointed to my
sign – "TRUTH JUSTICE KINDNESS" – and wondered what
part of this he had a problem with). I waved to the people
passing in cars – the support from the people in their cars really
inspired me – there were a lot of thumbs up and there were a
lot of horns being honked. At one point Salvation Army
volunteers came through with a wagon of free water and snacks
for the protesters – that was cool.

As I was leaving I stopped to thank the police officers for
coming and giving us their support and that's when I saw
Iris was there, too – she was chatting with the officers – and
they all let me take their photo.

There were also a few Trump supporters with rifles and pistols
and whatnot standing off to the side in a clump, and I took their
pictures, too.

White Privilege

If you
don't have to worry about looking suspicious
when you
walk around eating Skittles, wearing a hoodie
when you
go on a run through a suburban neighborhood
when you
carry assault rifles into a government building
then you
know white privilege
– Karen Molenaar Terrell

Floppy Copper Poppies

Floppy copper poppies hopping
in the breeze.
– Karen Molenaar Terrell

Fricasee Fracas Flummoxed

fricassee fracas flibbertigibbet flummoxed
prestidigitation preposterous obsequious
bovine blunderbuss balderdash brouhaha
cacophony kiester kerfuffle
discombobulated debacle
ubiquitous shenanigans hooligans
twitter-pated rutabaga gesundheit doh
– Karen Molenaar Terrell

I just felt it needed to be said.

June 6, 2020

Andrew: Are you going to take a picture of the sunset?
Karen: Yeah! I think it's going to be amazing tonight!
Andrew: Can I come along?
Karen: Yeah! Let's do this!

June 7, 2020

Shopping at Fred Meyer's this morning. There was an interesting feeling in there. Kind of edgy. When I went through the checkout I saw one of my old students was doing the bagging – Kayla with the Cheerful Heart. Kayla is ALWAYS smiling, and usually laughing. I found myself smiling just to see her there, working her magic. I asked her (muffled through my mask) how she was doing and she said she and the cashier had been yelled at a lot this morning – I looked over to the cashier and she nodded her head in confirmation. I wondered out loud what was going on with people right now. "It's Sunday," I said half to myself, trying to work it out, "Maybe people are just coming from church." (I'd noticed the church parking lots were full this morning.) Kayla and the checker started laughing out loud, nodding their heads, agreeing that THAT was probably what was happening.

Then Kayla said this was the first day in months she hadn't worn a mask – she'd been starting to feel sick because she'd had to wear a mask for months on the job and it was making her asthma act up. She said one of the customers had yelled at her for not wearing a mask. The cashier nodded her head – she'd just taken her mask off for a moment to talk to someone when the same customer had started yelling at her, too.

Sheesh.

I turned to the guy behind me in line – he wasn't wearing a mask. I pointed to my smiley masked face and asked him if he could tell I was smiling under my mask. He laughed and said yeah. I asked him if anyone had yelled at him this morning because he wasn't wearing a mask (probably half the folks in the store weren't wearing masks today) – and he laughed and said no, he just did "this" (and he showed me a cranky-looking frown) and people mostly avoided him. I started cracking up. I agreed the frown probably worked wonders in those kinds of social "situations."

My groceries all packed up in paper bags, Kayla and the checker lady – and the unmasked guy behind me – all wished me a good day and I moved on.

As I walked out of the store I started thinking about the whole masked/unmasked thing. I wear a mask when I'm in supermarkets and public places because I figure it's the least I can do right now to help the folks around me. When I consider what generations before me had to sacrifice as they went through World Wars and the Great Depression a mask doesn't seem like a big deal to me. BUT I am not going to judge other people's choices about that. It seems silly, to me, to let masks (or no masks) define people or determine their worth and value.

We're all dealing with a lot of challenges right now – financial challenges, social isolation, concerns about health and politics. People are stressed. People are scared. And, for some people, fear presents itself as anger, indignation, self-righteousness, quick tempers and impatience. I'm going to make an effort not to be one of those people – but I'm also going to make an effort to understand and be patient with my fellow humans who find themselves snapping and angry and indignant. It ain't easy being human. I'm going to trust that we're all doing the best we can.

If ever there was a time to give each other grace, it is now.

He Underestimated the People

He underestimated the goodness
of the people of this country.
And that was his downfall.
– Karen Molenaar Terrell

Andrew: Shall we go find the sunset?
Karen: I'm in!

June 16, 2020

Without going into detail about what was going on here, my eldest son just witnessed me talking to a customer service rep on the phone. During the course of the conversation the customer rep asked me my full name. I told her I was really embarrassed to give her my first name now because of the meme, but I promised her I wasn't going to want to talk to her manager. Andrew could hear her laughing through the phone. We had a delightful conversation and she helped me solve my problem and wished me a good day.

Andrew said he really enjoyed listening to how I talked to the rep. He said he witnessed me "dispelling myths and solving problems at the same time."

That felt good.

Honestly, though? Lately I've been struggling with the Karen meme a little. For years my Karen friends and I have marched, gone to rallies, written letters against bigotry and injustice, fought our own personal battles for equality – and now it feels like all that we've invested in equality – all our words and efforts – are being brushed aside like they never mattered to anyone or made any difference. The Karens – or maybe middle-aged women in general – are being lumped into one monolithic group and stereotyped – told by others what we believe – our own personal narratives taken from us and discounted.

And that really stinks.

Yesterday morning I read an article about a man who wrote "BLACK LIVES MATTER" on his own property and was chastised for doing that by a woman NAMED LISA who didn't believe him when he said it was his property. I was immediately indignant on this man's behalf – ready to share his story in my Facebook progressives group. And then I saw it. The news writer covering the story – a mainstream media writer named Madison Vanderberg – wrote: "The world is still protesting, marching, calling DA offices, signing petitions, and overhauling their social media presence in the name of civil rights and yet, despite all of this, Karens of the world are still calling the cops on people of color." And a little further on the man himself – the very man who had been a victim of bigotry – referred to the woman NAMED LISA as a "Karen." (It is interesting to note that no label was attached to the woman's husband – who was also present.)

And seriously?

I found myself shutting down – just staring at the screen and trying to process what the hell I'd just read there.

And here's the thing: Exchanging one target of bigotry for another is not progress, you know?

Let me share some of the stories of the Karens who are my friends:

Karen Blair Troianello was a gifted runner, born at a time when females did not have equal opportunity to participate in school sports. She changed that: "Troianello is more than a passionate advocate of sports for girls. She is a pioneer who left her name — her maiden name — forever etched in state history. She is

the former Karen Blair, the named plaintiff in the landmark
Blair v. Washington State University lawsuit in 1979 that
forced greater gender equity in college athletics." (Ringer,
Sally. "Female Athletes Have Blair to Thank." "Seattle Times,"
June 22, 2012.
https://www.spokesman.com/stories/2012/jun/22/female-
athletes-have-blair-to-thank/).

Because of Karen Blair Troianello equity was legislated for
females in school sports. Let's show her some appreciation.

My friend Karen Beckner has long fought for equality – here's
a photo of her in "The Skagit Valley Herald," marching for the
rights of migrant children.

My friend Karen Rippberger ran for public office as a
progressive in a conservative district in Oregon, and – although
she didn't win the election – she's played a part in helping her
local LGBTQ community's battle for equal rights. Laura
Camacho wrote in her voter's guide: "Karen Rippberger has a
servant's heart approach to leadership that is palpable on her
website."

And here are pictures of me - a giddy Karen standing with
Cory Booker at the 2012 state Democratic convention; a
fuchsia-hatted Karen marching in the 2017 women's march;
and a sign-holding Karen at our local BLM rally.

Trust me – you want the Karens who are my friends fighting on
your side. The Karens who are my friends don't put up with
bigotry, inequity, stereotypes, ageism, racism, sexism,
discrimination, or lazy labels.

Peggy Bissell writes: *Stereotyping people is one of the first steps in discrimination.*

Leslie S. writes: *Thank you for putting into words what so many of us wish we could.*

Allen N. writes: *You seem to me to fit the meme perfectly: Karen, to Lady Liberty: "Excuse me, but I'd like to speak to your manager regarding some complaints that I have...." Not all complaints to management are signs of "privilege". Especially when you are seeking to get OTHER people the same privileges that you have.*

XY writes: *The way I see it, no one is hating on individual Karens. The name is being used as a symbol of white women who use white privilege to get their way. I just posted recently that I am Karen, we all are. It is not something we should be denying or be defensive about. We white women benefit from white supremacy and we need to recognize it and take action. The use of "Karen" is being used to wake up white women, not bully them. I see "Karen" as an educational campaign, and it's working. It's creating conversation, like this one.*

Linda F. writes: *XY, Our words and our labels matter.*

Susan H. writes: *I completely agree with you, Linda!*

Karen Z. writes: *Thank you for posting something. I honestly have been starting to think I should change my name. I am so over this karen meme thing. And the fact that journalists are using it makes it worse.*

Katie G. writes: *I should add I totally agree there should be NO sweeping generalizations that stigmatize or negatively* *characterize any group of people. As a white friend/ally who has been sticking her neck out on behalf of others for a long time, I'm bristling at the "where have you white folks been hiding all this time, and I know you're just doing this now bcuz it makes you look good" comments. Not helpful. It takes some backbone to ignore those and continue on. Many people don't realize, a lot of us women have been dealing with negative stereotyping, not to mention harassment and discrimination, for our whole lives, too. But going around saying "men are jerks" would be largely untrue, and wholly counterproductive. Positive energy is what fuels positive change!*

Jeff Chase writes*: There are some that will always fear strong, independent women. They're mostly weak men that see their power slipping and feel their ignorance exposed. Ignore them, their time is running out. Keep fighting for equality. We need your courage, your wisdom, and your kindness now more than ever. I'm proud to stand with you all.*

For My Labeled Friends

'A rose by any other name would smell as sweet'
and bigotry of whatever kind will always stink.
– Karen Molenaar Terrell

Shaming

Let's stop shaming each other,
stop blaming each other –
stop looking for the faults and flaws
in each other.
No human is perfect –
we've all made mistakes –
let's stop pointing fingers
and each do what it takes
to tear down the walls,
and set free the doves
celebrate our differences
and practice Love's love.
– Karen Molenaar Terrell

June 21, 2020

It is Father's Day – and it is also my dad's 102nd birthday – a double whammy. When Dad was 99 and lying in a hospital bed with a UTI, angry that he wasn't being allowed to leave, he announced to my husband and me that he was "going to live to be 102!"

He almost made it, too. He died January 19th of this year – just five months short of his goal.

A lot has happened in those five months. If my dad were suddenly to reappear here today and look around at what's happened to our world in the last five months I'm not sure what he'd make of it all. I know he'd be celebrating some of it – I know he'd support the Black Lives Matter movement and be glad to see the progress that is being made towards equality for all people. He'd probably be baffled to see everyone walking around in face masks – but I think he'd like the smiley face on mine. He might be frustrated by the way elderly folks are being isolated from the community and he probably wouldn't like not being able to have a lot of visitors. But – as he always managed to do – he'd make the best of the circumstances – he'd rejoice in the good, patiently wait for the bad stuff to pass, and remain hopeful about the future. He was born at the end of WWI and the beginning of the Spanish Flu pandemic; survived the Great Depression and service in WWII; and survived ten days in a small tent in a blizzard at 25,000' on K2 – he wouldn't be daunted by 2020. Pffft.

My dad, Dee Molenaar, had a full and wonderful 101 years and seven months. He saw his share of tragedies, but he also saw his share of triumphs.

I miss him. As I look at the photo of him, standing next to my mother on their wedding day, I feel him with me. I feel them both with me. Giving me courage. Telling me it's all going to be alright. We'll make it through this.

Happy Father's Day, Daddy.

June 25, 2020

I found another treasure while sorting through my piles and cupboards during the COVID-19 lockdown: the memory of an old friend.

I found the memory as I was going through the shelves and more shelves and stacks of books I've accumulated through a lifetime of reading. I have books from my sci-fi phase; from my fantasy phase; from my romance phase; from my mystery phase; from my memoirs phase; from my true life adventures phase. I have books from authors who make me laugh and books by authors who make me think, and books by authors who make me do both. There's my Tolkien collection and my Vonnegut collection and my Douglas Adams collection and my old Earl Emerson collection. There are my Neil Gaiman books and my Norah Roberts books and my Jane Austin books and my Agatha Christie books. And, as I was sorting through my stacks, I found I'd accumulated a whole lot of Christian Science books, too – and that's when I stumbled upon the memory of my friend.

I'd come upon yet another copy of *Science and Health with Key to the Scriptures* by Mary Baker Eddy – this one was a "Reader's Edition" – an old black leather beauty. I opened it up to see if I could find out where I'd come by this one – and that's when I saw – written in elegant red calligraphy – the name of my dear friend, Jane Elofson. Just seeing her name there awakened a sweet memory of my friend's beautiful smile.

Jane Elofson had been one of the people who had made me feel welcome when my husband and I moved to Skagit County 35 years ago and I began attending the local Christian Science church. Jane, and her husband, Gordon, must have been about 68 or 69 then. They were one of those couples from The Greatest Generation that exuded a kind of classy kindness and grace. Gordon was handsome and dignified without being stuffy – he had a wonderful laugh and a great sense of humor. And Jane was stylish and gracious and funny – she had a "Ginger Rogers" kind of class about her.

As I stared at Jane's name in the book I couldn't remember when I'd last seen Gordon and Jane – and when I'd lost contact with them. It'd been decades, at least.

I thought it might be cool if I could do some googling and see if I could find some children, or maybe grandchildren, that I could send Jane's book to. I imagined her loved ones opening up my package and finding Jane's name in the book, and I imagined the happy surprise that might bring them. But there was little information to glean from the internet about Gordon and Jane. There was a 1940 census that placed them in Oregon when they were both 23 and newly-married. There were possible obituaries in Minnesota and an old photo of what might have been a younger version of Jane. But, eventually, I hit a dead end on the World Wide Web.

I contacted a mutual friend who had loved the Elofsons, too, and she gave me a bit more information – she told me she thought the Elofsons had a son, an artist, who lived on the east coast somewhere. I went back to googling, but soon stalled out again.

In the end, it seems the only physical evidence I have to show that Jane Elofson was ever on this planet is her elegant signature in the leather-bound copy of the *Science and Health* I found in my stacks of books.

Maybe this is what she would have wanted. Maybe there's something kind of clean and simple about leaving this planet with no trace of yourself – no trace that you ever lived on it, or were ever a part of it.

But I can't help myself – I feel a real yearning to call out Jane's name at least this one more time – to bring her name to the World Wide Web and acknowledge her existence – acknowledge her kindness to me and remember her beautiful smile.

June 30, 2020

Back in February and March – when COVID-19 was first making the news – I had terrible fears for a loved one who was traveling through Europe. My terror caused me to pull out all the tools I'd acquired in my life to get me through troubling times – and one of the chief tools was expressing gratitude for all the good in my life.

I remember lying in bed one night in particular – my thoughts were all agitated and I couldn't find peace. I was just staring at the ceiling, trying to calm myself, and I started listing in my thoughts all the people I was grateful for in my life – my sons, husband, Mom and Dad, siblings, nieces and nephews, in-laws, friends from grade school, junior high, high school, university, Mount Rainier friends, neighbors, colleagues, church friends, Amazon Forum Humoristian friends, FB friends, WordPress friends – and then I found myself including people who might not be considered "friends" – people I thought had maybe treated me unkindly or unfairly, people I'd had a rift with – and I found myself genuinely grateful for THEM, too, and for my connection to them.

It was a cosmic moment for me. I felt my connection to all of Love's creation – and each and every expression of Life. I knew this overwhelming gratitude that I'm not solitary and alone in this vast, infinite universe – grateful for my connection to all the infinite expressions of Life. I felt Love's presence with me – supporting me – sure and comforting and healing and powerful. My fears dissolved away and I was able to go back to sleep.

I'm going to practice having more of those cosmic moments.

And I know those moments begin with love.

The Good Works Competition?

Karen writes: Black lives matter more than statues. Living human beings matter more than stone idols of dead people.

A.D.W. writes: And yet, if all this energy and anger were directed to actually saving black lives from crime and murder in S Chicago, Baltimore, and Detroit - our urban Liberal run cities - I might care about a statue memorializing someone's life greater than the part slavery played in it. We are all larger than our flaws. So add a plaque. We should cancel the Cleveland Indians not because it's derogatory but because of the common use of slaves in native America. There are people TONIGHT held in slavery and trafficking worldwide. Where's the ACTION behind ENDING SLAVERY?? Then think about a stupid statue. How about that?

I am involved in ending human trafficking here in Michigan. Are you???

Karen writes: I think it's great that you are involved in ending human trafficking.

You ask: "Where's the ACTION behind ENDING SLAVERY?? Then think about a stupid statue. How about that?"

And exactly. Why would anybody make the protection of statues the priority right now? Why would our president make the protection of statues his priority when there's human trafficking, children separated from their parents at the border, Black men being lynched, and being killed by officers of the law, the planet is being destroyed, there's a global pandemic, and etc?

I get the sense that you want to know what I've been doing to help humanity and then comparing that to the good you've done in ending human trafficking? Are you... is this a competition of some kind? I think we've talked about this before. I am a teacher. I spent the last seven years of my career working with a mostly minority population in a nonprofit alternative high school for 1/3 of the pay I got as a public school teacher. I didn't do this because I thought I was in some kind of "good works" competition. I did this work because I knew I was making a positive difference in the lives of young people and that felt good to me, intrinsically. I loved the students I worked with - they were wonderful people who'd already experienced more challenges in their young lives than most of us ever will.

July

PORTLAND (Reuters) - As a U.S. Navy veteran, Chris David said he thought he would be able to talk plainly with federal agents in Portland and ask them why they were using unmarked cars to snatch people off the street during recent protests in the Oregon city. When he tried to speak with them outside the federal courthouse in Portland on Saturday night, he said a federal officer beat him with a baton, breaking his hand in two places. A second officer sprayed him with chemical irritant, David said.

"I wanted to ask them 'Why are you guys not following the Constitution?' But we never got there," David said in an interview. "They whaled on me like a punching bag."

A video appearing to show David being beaten by a federal officer and sprayed with a chemical by another while he stood passively went viral this weekend with 10.7 million views.

- Bloom, Deborah. "Navy Veteran Says He Was Beaten Like a Punching Bag in Portland." Reuters, 20 July, 2020. (https://www.reuters.com/article/us-global-race-protests-portland-veteran/navy-veteran-says-he-was-beaten-like-a-punching-bag-in-portland-idUSKCN24L2CP)

It Is Beyond Me at This Point

So I had three pairs of reading glasses. Lost pairs #1 and #2 months ago. Bought pair #4. Lost pair #3 a couple days ago - right after I bought pair #4. Just now - as I was sitting in my office - the thought came to me to look in this pile of papers beside my desk - I thought I'd remembered hearing something drop from my desk the other day - maybe, I thought, it was pair #3. So I sort of pushed things aside and found pair #2. No. I don't know. It is beyond me at this point. Maybe Life is playing some kind of weird hat trick with me...? I'll probably find pair #3 in the refrigerator or something. I've found socks in there before.

Alrighty. That is all. Carry on then...

Elizabeth E. Fisher writes: *Socks in the fridge? Remind me not to come for a meal!*

July 1, 2020

The Terrell Brothers are making music. Andrew is on piano.
Xander on drums. This is what a "lock-down" looks like in the
Terrell home. The sons bring me such joy!

July 3, 2020

I just had a flashback from 40 years ago. I was on a ferry from Seattle to Bremerton – I think I'd been visiting a friend in Seattle. I was standing at the railing of the ferry by myself, looking out over the water. A good-looking young man with blue eyes approached me and started chatting. He was visiting from another state, he said. Out here to lead a meeting or a gathering – I don't remember his exact words now. He thought I might be interested in going to this meeting. I asked him what it was about. He said he was with the KKK. I remember feeling like I'd just been kicked in the gut – thinking he did not look like what I thought a KKK member would look like – shocked that there was anyone in the KKK in Washington State – wasn't the KKK a southern thing?

I told him no, I was not interested in his meeting. He tried to convince me to join him. I remember saying something like: "The KKK is against rights for Blacks. The KKK hates Black people." And he smiled this really charming smile and said that no, the KKK wasn't about hating Black people – the KKK just wanted to make sure White people had rights, too – or something like that. I told him no, the KKK is racist, and no, I was not going to go to his meeting, and I walked away.

And here we are. Forty years later. My heart is breaking.

July 4, 2020

Saw a white goose hanging out with a gaggle of Canada geese
today. I thought that was pretty cool. Made me think of that
white buffalo prophecy. So I created my own prophecy:

The Prophecy of the Snow-White Goose

And in the day when the snow-white goose shall appear
amongst the Canada geese and slurp seaweed
and honketh together as family – in that day shall we
see how all creatures should live together
and in that day shall we know harmony.
– Karen Molenaar Terrell

July 6, 2020

Long long ago and in a land far far away I stumbled into a
rabbit hole full of delightful misfits and smartasses, wise folk
and wits, and wacky and wonderful hooligans - the original
Humoristians. My life would never be the same.

It was the summer of 2007. I was checking out my book on
Amazon and saw that there were discussion forums listed at the
bottom of the page. I clicked on one of the links and found a
land full of rousing and intriguing conversations about Big
Ideas – it was just like being back in university again. We
talked about God and Nogod and The Bible and world leaders
and policies and policy-makers and writers and books. As we
bounced ideas off each other – shared and listened, debated and
learned from each other – and laughed! – we built bonds of
friendship and kinship that have lasted to this day.

As time goes on, I've come to realize just how valuable and
important that time in the Amazon forums was for me. I
learned so much from my Amazon friends!

A good chunk of my Facebook friends are friends from the
Amazon forums. And a lot of them have become friends to my
other friends, too! And I've become friends to THEIR friends
and family. The ripples keep extending.

In the last few years we've begun to lose some of our Amazon
classmates. Randy Kercher died unexpectedly in 2017. Dean
Wrzeszcz died of COVID-19 in April. I feel like I've lost
family.

And I guess Randy's death and Dean's death have given me a sense of urgency about letting my Amazon friends know how important they are to me. How much I love them. How grateful I am to have met them. We shared a unique and wonderful time together. My theistic heart believes we were meant to meet there and meant to be friends. Look at all we've come through together in the last 13 years! I've felt your support through the challenging times. I've been so grateful for your humor on those days when I really needed a good laugh. I've been so grateful for your wisdom on those days when I needed a new perspective. I can't imagine my life now without you in it.

Thank you, dear friends.

(Through the years I've actually been able to meet some of my Amazon friends in the person: Kathi and Jamie in Nova Scotia; Marissa in Minnesota; Becky in Virginia; David in Michigan; and Allen N., and Heather and her family, Craig and his wife, and Marissa and her husband, David and his family, and Sandra and her husband, have all taken the time to meet up with me in western Washington State. What a joy!)

Found an old journal from probably 40 years ago as I was sorting through old boxes and bins.

I opened it up and found this word-doodle left by my young self: "Even if ten years from now you're not the same person, this person that you were really existed and lived. Love and trust and beauty aren't magical – they're real – and you can take them with you wherever you go. Be happy that you're alive for this one moment of peace and contentment when you have everything you need."

I think I needed the voice of my younger self speaking to me today from the before-times.

Black Lives Matter More Than Statues

Black lives matter more than statues.
Living human beings matter more
than stone idols. The victims used
to mock and shame matter more
than the cheap laugh someone gets
from a vicious campaign.
Children separated from parents
matter more than The Wall. The health
of our planet matters more than
the wealth of CEOs. Women matter
even when they're not incubators.
LGBTQ rights matter more
than the hate of the haters.
– Karen Molenaar Terrell

July 13, 2020

One happy story has emerged from the Slug Battles this summer: The Story of the Intrepid Little Sunflower.

The slugs and snails have been voracious this year. When my little sunflowers first sprouted I covered them every night with jars. When they outgrew the jars I would sometimes wake up in the middle of the night and go on Slug Patrol – looking for any snails or slugs that might be chowing down on my sunflower youngsters (in the morning I would take the slugs and snails out to our wetland – what I've dubbed my "Snail and Slug Refuge" – and ask them to please stay down there). Eventually I started wrapping copper tape around the bottom of the sunflowers' stems and that seemed to work pretty well – UNTIL one morning I found a slug or snail had chomped through the stem of one of the sunflower youngsters and the top three inches were hanging from the bottom three inches by mere threads. I tried to tape it together, but that didn't work well. Finally, I pulled the top part off and – finding I didn't have it in me to toss it in the compost – I put it in a little bottle filled with water and put it on top of a book case, and waited for nature to take its course.

But the little sunflower did not die. In fact, it appeared to me that she even grew a few inches.

A couple weeks went by and the leaves started turning yellow. It was obvious to me my little sunflower teenager needed nutrients. On impulse, I put about half an inch of soil in the bottom of the bottle and made sure the bottom of the sunflower stem touched the soil – I hoped the plant would somehow suck up the nutrients it needed – maybe it would grow roots? I wasn't sure how that worked – but it seemed possible to me.

And today when I looked over at the sunflower teenager she seemed to have grown six inches overnight! I looked at the bottom of the bottle and there were roots in there!

I planted her in a planter out on the deck. Right now she is out there, straight and getting taller, and waving happily in the breeze at me.

July 20, 2020

We went back to Mount Rainier last weekend to spread Dad's ashes, per his wishes, "on the highest point on Alta Vista." It was a wonderful weekend with family. There was still a lot of snow up there, so we were a little limited in hiking trails - but we managed a couple short hikes - I hiked with Scott along the top of Mazama Ridge, and did a quick hike with Andrew around Longmire and then up a trail next to the road that goes to Paradise. We also all hiked up to Alta Vista from Paradise, of course, to spread Dad's ashes on the highest point. One marmot seemed particularly interested in what we were about up there - he was very cute - posed on a boulder for us and sniffed in our direction to make sure we behaved ourselves under his supervision.

At the end of the weekend, as we sat socially-distanced on the patio at the Jimmy Beech House and shared Dad-stories, a breeze swirled in a circle around us - enveloping us in the fragrance of the forest. I could feel Moz and Dad in the breeze - celebrating with us - surrounding us in love and joy.

It's done, Dad. You're safe on your mountain at last.

July 24, 2020

Message to a friend -

Plato told us to "be kind, for everyone you meet is fighting a hard battle." I know some of the battles my friends on here have been through that you know nothing about. I've been through my own battles that I don't feel comfortable sharing on a public thread. I'm going to assume YOU are going through your own battles, too - probably dealing with stuff that I know nothing about - and that is what is giving me some restraint here. I am busy enough dealing with my own flaws and foibles to have time to spend working on someone else's.

But some of the things you've said on my threads have, frankly, horrified me - you seem to think it's alright for federally-funded storm troopers - people my tax dollars have employed! - to round up innocent protesters, beat them, and detain them unlawfully - and that is... I can't even wrap my head around it. You have implied American citizens should stop using their constitutional rights because federal thugs have become violent towards them. And no - what should happen there is that the federal thugs should be the ones removed from the streets - not the protesters. In my mind, you have it backasswards - the thugs shouldn't be in control; the law-abiding citizens should.

I am tired, my friend. Worn down by the insanity. After reading your comments and other comments by other friends on other threads, I am losing hope for my country. The last three years have exposed to me things about the people I consider "friends" that... I am, frankly, shocked and disheartened by the callous disregard for other people; the hate-mongering and fear-mongering; and the fact that some of my friends are okay with storm troopers in our streets, bullying my fellow citizens.

What has happened to common decency? To caring for one another? To reaching out a hand to those in need of support? To standing up together against bullies and bigots and thugs? What has happened to the Golden Rule?

July 26, 2020

I have two friends - Paul Swortz and Josh Fielder - who are veterans and in Portland right now, making a wall to protect the BLM protesters. Paul is in this "New York Post" photo - he's the one in the gold helmet and red handkerchief.

Paul and Josh - I think you guys may be standing near each other in the line. Josh - look for the fellow in the gold helmet.

You are heroes.

Paul Swortz writes*: The camera adds 10 pounds, and there were at least four cameras on me, apparently.*

July 28, 2020

"The sense of identity is the root of all suffering."
-Mooji

Karen to Andrew: I've lost my parents; I've lost my youth; I'm
losing my hearing; I've lost my beauty; I'm not a teacher
anymore; now even my name stinks.
Andrew: You know what comes next?
Karen: The grave?
Andrew: (Laughing.) Nah, you get closer to God.

Your true identity does not depend upon
a job title or a five-star review or your age
or the money in your bank account
or how many followers you have on your page
or your gender, weight, height, skin color, or name,
or your religion, political party, family or fame.
Your true identity is eternally held and maintained
safe in Love and Truth, free from shame.
– Karen Molenaar Terrell

I just had a HUGE breakthrough, my friends! Lately I'd found
myself feeling some negative bias towards people who used
my name as a synonym for a white supremacist anti-mask
Trump supporter. I'd come to believe that those who use
"Karen" as a pejorative were not original thinkers, tended
towards bigotry, were prone to labeling and stereotypes,
enjoyed deriding and laughing at others, were bullies, and were
unkind. BUT…

NONE OF THAT is the truth about ANY of us! If I accept that lie about even ONE of God's children, I am allowing myself to get pulled into a whole tangled rat's nest of nonsense – that, in the end, is going to bring me nothing good.

"When we identify ourselves with the sense of personhood, we are much like a wave on the surface of the ocean. Rather than resting in the vast space of pure Being, we become identified with some kind of passing event, thought, or emotion – perhaps a wave of anger, a particular role in our life, or even our entire sense of personhood."
– Mooji, Vaster Than Sky, *Greater Than Space*

"Grown-ups love figures… When you tell them you've made a new friend they never ask you any questions about essential matters. They never say to you 'What does his voice sound like? What games does he love best? Does he collect butterflies?' Instead they demand 'How old is he? How much does he weigh? How much money does his father make?' Only from these figures do they think they have learned anything about him."
– Antoine de Saint-Exupery, *The Little Prince*

July 29, 2020

I found ten perfect minutes today - sitting in the shade outside the coffee shop - all alone in the space set aside for patrons, sipping my blueberry-spinach-coconut milk smoothie. I watched the sailboats and paddle boarders and kayakers gliding by on the bay - and, with my mask securely fastened about my face - asked a pair of friends who've known each other for 40 years if I could take their photo for them - they said yes and thank you. Another pair of friends - a Black woman and a White woman - walked by and stopped on the walk in front of me to look out at the water - and I had to comment on the beautiful sweater one of the friends was wearing - she smiled and thanked me and told me she ordered her sweater online. Just as I was contemplating leaving and continuing on with my walk a family came out of the coffee shop and joined me in the space for patrons - my table was the only one in the shade, and I told them that I was leaving and they could sit where I was. They smiled and - making sure to keep the proper social distance - we moved around each other and they took over the table out of the sun.

Ten perfect minutes is a pretty wonderful thing.

That Phrase Kind of Freaked Me Out, Too

Karen writes*: A couple of friends have talked about the rioting and violence that have occurred at some of the Black Lives Matter protests. I've been responding individually to their comments, but I thought it might save me time if I just did a copy and paste of my last response to a friend and saved it here:*

Yeah. I hear you. CHOP in Seattle was a mess - I ain't going to disagree with you there. But... if you scroll down my wall you'll see an interesting post about who's actually been causing the mayhem - and, according to the "Washington Post," it is apparently not "antifa" - it's been caused mostly by "local hooligans, sometimes gangs, sometimes just individuals that are trying to take advantage of an opportunity." According to the article, the alt-right "Boogaloo" movement has played a part in the violence, too. (Kelly, Meg. Samuels, Elyse. "Who Caused the Violence at Protests? It Wasn't Antifa." "Washington Post," 22 June, 2020.)

From my own experience participating in the local BLM rally in Burlington, the only maybe threatening and intimidating element I saw there were the half a dozen Trump supporters standing off to the side with their rifles, self-appointed to "keep the peace." The actual police officers there - whom I thanked for their support - were very calm and friendly - and the protest was entirely peaceful.

The racism and hate crimes in this country need to end. Now. None of us who are true Americans can allow it to continue for even one more day. And when the bulk of our president's Fourth of July speech is loaded with division and hate for his own constituents - instead of the compassion and understanding we all sorely need right now - we need to call him on it.

Sandy R. writes: *Our local cops are heroes. Yes, there are bad cops out there. That one percent that needs to be dealt with. But how is defunding 50 percent even remotely reasonable? Can someone even convince me? Our local cops are understaffed big time. I'm all for equality. I'm all for BLM and every other life that matters, but how in the hell did we get to this point? And I can assure you that in two years people will be screaming "why didn't I get an emergency response?"*

Karen writes: *Honestly, that phrase "defunding the police" kind of freaked me out at first, too - and then I thought I'd do a google search to find out what that actually means. Here's what I found:*

"'Defund the police' means reallocating or redirecting funding away from the police department to other government agencies funded by the local municipality. That's it. It's that simple. Defund does not mean abolish policing..." (Ray, Rashawn. "What Does Defund the Police Mean and Does It Have Merit?" brookings.edu, 19 June, 2020.)

Sandy R. writes: *You can spin it in any way you want. Fine, take that money and reallocate it. Again, in two years when we don't get emergency response, guess what...crickets. People are begging for police to get more training. Throw that out the window just like the baby in the bath water. Forget that now the cops won't have any time to be community engagement* *activists that check in on businesses and schools. You can forget all of it when you take that funding away. Thank GOD my husband retired in January because I would even be more pissed than I am right now. By the way...where were all of you five years ago?*

Karen writes*: I'm guessing you didn't actually read the article?*

Sandy R. writes*: I did read it. Days ago. Want to get ahold of a mental health professional in the middle of the night when the person is out of control and not only endangering a person or themselves? Good luck. You going to leave the ER crew with an out-of-hand person? Good luck. Have you gone on a cop ride-along?*

Karen writes*: Where was I five years ago? Teaching at a local alternative high school - working with a mostly minority population of students - working with a lot of students who have experienced bigotry and discrimination first-hand. I felt really blessed to be able to be a part of the work there.*

Sandy R. writes*: So if a person invades your home with a gun and threatens your life do you call 911 or a mental health professional?*

Karen writes*: THAT is when you call 911. When your student is having a mental health crisis - talking about suicide - do you call 911 or a mental health professional?*

It's been lovely chatting with you - and I think I understand where you're coming from - but it is 11:17 and time for me to get these old bones to bed.

You and I are not enemies here, you know. I think we probably actually want the same things for our world.

Sandy R. writes: *You know I love you. This does not come from hate. It comes from compassion and knowing what my hubby has dealt with for 27 years. I am the wife of a cop and military man. I know what he sees. I have seen a small part of what he has seen. We need equal ground and we all know that. But don't throw away what resources these officers provide. It's huge.*

August

The Trump administration continued its attacks on the U.S. Postal Service and voting rights Thursday, as President Donald Trump admitted he is denying USPS funding to block mail-in voting while White House economic adviser Larry Kudlow called voting rights "not our game"—prompting an outcry from Democrats alleging Trump is "sabotaging" the election through his continued politicization of the postal service.

Trump, a longtime USPS critic who has falsely claimed mail-in voting will lead to voter fraud despite a lack of evidence, said Thursday that he's holding up a stimulus deal over Democratic demands for funding to USPS and for mail-in voting, saying Democrats "need that money in order to make the post office work so it can take all of these millions and millions of ballots."

Durkee, Alison. "Trump Admits to Blocking USPS Funding Over Mail-In Voting, Biden Slams Move as 'Pure Trump'."Forbes, 13 August, 2020 (Trump admits to blocking usps funding over mail-in voting)

The Kitty Is on My Head

Clara Kitty just put her little paw on the side of my face and brought her nose to my nose. Kitty kisses.

The kitty is on my head now. Just thought you would want to know.

Alrighty. Carry on then...

Elizabeth E. Fisher writes: *You are a fashion statement!*

August 1, 2020

I have such a weird life. Spooned some of Dad's ashes into a sandwich bag and then put that into an empty Pirouline's cookie canister tube and then in a cardboard box. Took the box to the post office and sent it off priority mail to a climbing friend of Dad's who's going to take it to the summit of Rainier.

Waved good bye to Dad's ashes as I walked out of the post office.

August 2, 2020

I sat at a picnic table near the children's play area at Boulevard
Park and watched people being awesome and doing good
things. There was Susanne, picking up the litter she found ("I
was a Girl Scout," she said. "Old habits die hard"). And there
were Ashley (with her pup, Okanee) and Trista sitting on a
couple of benches below me, becoming new friends across a
socially-safe distance. And there were parents getting their
children outside for fresh air and sunshine. And youngsters,
Alden and Ducklin, carrying around a log that they just really
liked. And old friends chatting and laughing together. I felt
inspired by my fellow beings today.

August 3, 2020

So I've been pretty much wearing black for the last five months. Although I'd like to say that I've been doing this in protest or something – it's really just because I've not had any interest in my clothes. I have, like, five black tops and I just rotate them over my black shorts or my black jeans and I don't spend much time thinking about it. But today it occurred to me that maybe that's affecting my psyche. Maybe I should make some effort. So I put on a purple top; Put on my new capri blue jeans; I EVEN went so far as to put on a pair of dangly earrings – and my smiley mask, of course. And then I got myself in the car and drove to Sisters Espresso and showed off myself to Brooke. "See? See?" I mumbled through my mask, "I'm not wearing black today?! And see – I've got new capri pants! And I'm even wearing earrings!!!" Brooke (I so love her!) gave me the exactly right feedback and encouragement I needed for making an effort.

I ordered a lavender green iced tea for myself, and then I looked across the espresso shop to the drive-thru window and yelled across to the bearded man, waiting patiently in his truck: "I'm buying you your drink today!" He smiled. "Sir, are you expensive?" I asked. He nodded his head yes and grinned. (His order wasn't expensive at all.) "I'm also taking your punch on my punch card," I informed him, pointing to my Sisters punch card, and he laughed.

And so ends another tale of derring do and adventure in the land of social distancing.

Ben T. writes*: I used to wear a lot of black. I was mourning, for sure. And then Covid-19 came along, and now I can be as colorful as I want. Got out of my stuffy office clothes and put something trashy on!*

Glad to see you're out giving Karens a good name, just like you always have.

Karen writes*: Ben, Triple "Love" for this one. I am so very glad you are on this planet with me, Admiralissimo Voodoo. And I really hope we can actually meet some day, dear friend! You can put on something trashy and I'll put on something with color in it and we'll celebrate ourselves.*

Karen: Sunset-hunter, you want to find one?
Andrew: Yeah. It looks like it's going to be a good one tonight!

August 4, 2020

The political signs are up now. Every time I drive by one of those "Keep America Great" signs I have a deep visceral reaction. I mean — seriously? — keep America great?! I don't know whether to laugh or cry. Or scream.

My country is in serious need of NOT keeping things as they are. We are in the midst of a pandemic — caused, in part, by a lack of political leadership. We have government agents in our streets — rounding up innocent protesters, beating and detaining them unlawfully as they try to practice their First Amendment rights. We have an environment that is being poisoned relentlessly by corporate greed. Racism is running rampant. Our constitution is threatened by the very person who took an oath to protect it.

We are in deep trouble here. And no, four more years of this is not the answer.

August 7, 2020

A friend said something in a comment that got me to thinking. (And that's a good thing, right?) She said that she didn't know a conversation she had participated in was going to "devolve into politics." I understand where she was coming from with that – I know not everyone is comfortable discussing politics. But I'd like to offer a different perspective.

The implication in my friend's comment was that discussing politics is a bad thing – maybe an uncivil thing? When something "devolves" it "degenerates" – "deteriorates, declines, sinks, slips, slides, worsens" (Google definition).

And I think it's a real tragedy that participating in a discussion about political issues and concerns – sharing our thoughts about things that matter to us, our community, our world – is considered a bad thing. I learn so much from these dialogues! If we live in a vacuum – separated from the thoughts and perspectives of others – how are we ever going to be able to know the problems and challenges our fellow earth-travelers are experiencing? How are we going to be able to reach out and help each other? How are we going to learn from each other and understand each other?

I know these kinds of discussions aren't enjoyable for everyone. And that's okay. I don't think anyone should be FORCED into sharing their beliefs. But I also don't think people should be made to feel they've somehow done something wrong by sharing their thoughts about stuff. I'm not going to apologize for wanting to talk about things that matter to me. The freedom we have to share our ideas and beliefs with each other is a part of what made America a place my grandparents wanted to immigrate to.

Dangling "to" – and I ain't apologizing for that, either.

August 8, 2020

Why do folks put guns and God – "gunsandGod" – together in the same breath like they're somehow connected – somehow equivalent? It makes no sense to me.

Guns and God. Turnips and God makes as much sense to me. If you love God, you must love turnips, too, right? Or… if you don't love turnips, you must not love God? Or… if you love turnips you must love guns…and God…? Eesh. Maybe it's all too deep for me to understand.

August 9, 2020

At the time it all seemed kind of matter-of-fact normal. I climbed Mount Hood at 15. Climbed Rainier the summer before I turned 21. Climbed Baker the summer before I turned 31. Climbed Adams the summer before I turned 41. And I felt challenged by these climbs, for sure – felt like I'd had to push myself to get to the tops of these peaks – but this is what the people around me did. I guess this was my "normal." It's not been until recently that the significance of those climbs has really hit me. And I'm kind of astounded by myself, to tell you the truth. I mean… who did I think I was that I would even CONTEMPLATE climbing those mountains?!!

I'm reading a book by Joe Wilcox right now about his climb of Denali back in 1967. He references Mount Rainier several times in his book – talks about how Rainier is often used to prepare climbers for major expeditions and how it's used to test the strength and ability of climbers to see if they are fit to climb in major expeditions. A lot of expedition climbers are from the Pacific Northwest because of their experience on Rainier. And most folks who come to Rainier to climb it have probably been preparing for that climb for months or even years. It is a big deal. Apparently.

Here's how I got to climb Rainier: I was working in the gift shop at Paradise – hiking around up there before and after work – my body was used to the altitude. I was sitting outside after work one evening – looking at the mountain. My friend, Perky Firch, who also worked at the Paradise Visitors Center, was sitting next to me. I said to her, "We're going to climb that mountain." She said okay. I called my dad to ask him if he could guide us to the summit, and he agreed to be our guide. Two weeks later we were standing on the top of Rainier.

And the sheer naive confidence of my young self – the fearless innocence of it all – astounds me!

What a blessed life I've enjoyed! What opportunities came from being Dee Molenaar's daughter! I don't think I fully appreciated that until now.

August 11, 2020

After Moz passed on, friends got together and sent me a young magnolia tree. Last summer - just before we left for our cross-country trip - I spotted its first bud - and I was a little sad that it bloomed while we were gone. This summer I've been looking for buds and haven't seen any - I finally gave up and figured it wasn't going to bloom this year. Then - just now! - I went outside and happened to look at the magnolia and it had a flower blooming on it! What a cool surprise!

***

A robin youngster ricocheted off our dining room window today as I was eating breakfast.

I ran outside and around to the window to see if I could help him. I looked below the window, thinking he'd maybe ended up there - but there was no trace of him. Then I looked through the rose bush next to the window and found him planted among the thorns. I was afraid he'd maybe gotten punctured by the spikes - at first I couldn't tell if he was alive - he was so still.

I ran to get some garden gloves to protect my hands and then went back to the rose bush and reached in to bring his little body out. This is when I realized he was still alive - he gratefully scooted into my hands and nestled inside them for a moment. When I opened my hands up to see how he was doing, he hopped on top of my finger and perched there for a while.

After he'd had a chance to recover a bit, I brought him next to a tree and he transferred himself from my finger to one of its branches. He didn't look injured - nothing seemed to be broken or bleeding. I think he's going to recover from this little adventure.

Fare thee well, my little friend!

August 17, 2020

So a month ago I decided to google myself. (Note to the wise:
DO NOT GOOGLE YOURSELF. EVER. FOR ANY
REASON.) What has come up in the past have been links to
my books, maybe some letters I wrote to newspapers, a link
to my blog, a couple stories about my dad. Stuff like that. And
I'm used to seeing four or five stars come up with my books.
And my ego has really enjoyed that.

But what has been coming up for the last month or so on the
first Google page of my search has been a one-star rating for an
audiobook I made of my book, *Blessings*. And that one-star
rating is stuck to that first page like a slug to my sunflowers.

A little background about my audiobook: Back in 2013 – after
one or two of my vision-challenged friends asked me to do this
– I used my husband's GarageBand app on his Mac and a
headphone and mic I bought for $29.95 at Best Buy to make an
audio recording of my book. Andrew showed me how to click
on stuff – showed me how to watch the sound-waves and
moderate the volume – and then patted me on the back and
wished me luck.

I never actually expected anyone to buy this thing – except
maybe those one or two friends who'd asked me to make it.
And I haven't thought much about it. I mean… until I found
the one-star rating on the front page of Google.

I know it's been good for me to find it there: It's nudged me to
contemplate what constitutes my true identity and value; to
snuggle in close to divine Love; and to spend some time in

self-reflection. And I've learned something about myself: At first, I was tempted to just delete the recording – but then I thought of the reason I'd made the recording in the first place – as an outreach to my friends who are struggling with their sight – so I sucked it up and kept the recording there. And I feel good about myself for that – for putting my friends ahead of my ego.

Anyway. Apparently Australia has its own audible.com audiobook site and yesterday I found some dear (and highly discerning) soul in Australia had given the exact same audio recording five stars all across the boards. Bless that person.

His Rival's Revival Rap

He thinks of the post office and his
constituents as his business rivals –
competition to be overcome and
not responsible for their survival –
But come November his "rivals"
will know a revival
and our country will go beyond tribal
survival.
– Karen Molenaar Terrell

Beyond Earth's Night

I woke up fretting
worries on my head
Looking up from my bed
and out the window
a lone star shone bright
connecting me to universal
infinite boundless light
reaching out to me
beyond earth's night.
– Karen Molenaar Terrell

August 18, 2020

Dear students –
Remember when we talked about the qualifications for
president? Remember what the qualifications are? Yes – good!
That's right! A person has to be a native-born American
citizen. Anything else? Yes! Right! A person has to be over 35,
and has to have lived in this country for at least 14 years.

So does everyone who is currently a candidate for president
and vice president meet those qualifications? Yup. Trump
(born in NY) and Pence (born in Indiana) and Biden (born in
Pennsylvania) and Harris (born in California) are all native-
born American citizens, are all over 35, and have all lived in
the U.S. for at least 14 years.

Now if you should encounter some weird post that calls any of
these candidates an "anchor baby" and, therefore, unable to be
president – or if you encounter an odd post about a conspiracy
designed to put someone else in the White House because one
of the candidates isn't qualified to be president – remember
what you learned in your eighth grade social studies class,
okay? You do not need to spend a lot of time "researching" this
stuff or even wondering about the possibility of it. You already
know what you need to know about this.
-Mrs. T.

August 19, 2020

I used some of my inheritance from Dad to bring solar energy to our home. I didn't want to just fritter away the inheritance - I wanted to do something with the inheritance that would honor both my parents. I think Dad and Mom would be happy I used the money in this way - the environment was important to both of them.

Here's a photo - our house wanted me to take a picture of it showing off its new solar panels. It is so proud.

August 20, 2020

Just got a phone call. It's 7:50 in the morning here. Who could it be? I pick up the phone.

Karen: Hello?

Man with heavily-accented voice: Hello. (Pause for several beats. I can hear a room full of voices on phones.)

Karen: What's this one going to be? Are you going to tell me my Pay Pal account has been suspended until I can provide documented proof of who I am? I'm going to prison if I don't immediately wire money to the IRS? My social security has been cancelled unless I give you my vital information?

Click. Line goes dead.

And so begins another day in America.

August 25, 2020

Please do not tell me what I believe, feel, and think.
– Do not assume because I am a progressive and tend to vote
for Democrats that I don't believe in God, "hate the Bible," and
want to kill babies and take away your guns.
– Do not assume because I believe in God that I am anti-
science, believe the earth is flat and the world was, literally,
created in seven days.
– Do not assume that because I'm white, middle-aged and
named "Karen" I am racist and want to talk to your manager.
– Do not assume that because I identify as a "Christian" I am
conservative, opposed to LGBTQ rights, opposed to women's
rights, travel heavily armed, and am voting for you-know-who.

I think if we see others in terms of stereotypes we miss out on
some beautiful friendships and kinship with our fellow
humans.

My biggest challenge right now is myself. I guess that's always
my biggest challenge, isn't it? Stay kind, Karen. Stay true.
Keep loving. Look for ways to bring humor to those in
desperate need of a good laugh. Don't hate. Never hate. Be
wise – but don't be cynical. Be discerning – but don't be cruel.

Love, help me be what you need me to be.
Amen.

They Came Home Last Night

They came home last night.
I was standing under the stars
as I waited for them – looking
up at the vast serene forever,
feeling Mom and Dad smiling
with me – and the car pulled up
into the driveway. I was hidden
in the darkness at first and they
didn't see me – then – "Have you
been waiting for us?" – and hugs
and laughter and so glad you're
home – gently emerging into the
here and now – and a paperclip
– Mom's special signal to me –
in the driveway. I pick it up and put
it in my pocket. I will add it to my
paperclip collection once I'm inside.
All together again.
– Karen Molenaar Terrell

August 28, 2020

I'm going to share this because I suspect other people might be feeling the same way. I want you to know you're not alone.

Lately I've found myself beginning to detach from the world. I don't mean this in a melodramatic or suicidal way - but lately I've felt like I don't belong here anymore. I feel like I've done everything I needed and wanted to do here. I brought two wonderful sons into the world, and helped escort two wonderful parents out of the world; I've climbed the mountains I wanted to climb; had a fulfilling career teaching some really amazing young people; wrote some books and took some photos and sang some songs. I have had a really wonderful life.

But now I look around at the world I'm living in and I'm just not sure I fit here anymore, you know? I feel like maybe I'm just taking up space, in the way, an annoyance - like I have no business being here and certainly no business talking to anyone's manager.

It's wearing: The hate; the division; the shameless racism and sexism and generationalism; and the blatant and unending lies and dishonesty coming from the man who should be leading us - and my fellow citizens applauding him! - and telling me I'm "not of sound mind" because I DON'T applaud him!

Yeah, I've lived long enough to know that things CAN get better - that there IS progress - that sometimes we have to walk through the manure to get to where we want to be. I guess that's what's kept me going.

But right now - in this moment - I feel myself detaching.

I am weary of the world.

August 29, 2020

I love this man. Charles Atkinson is one of the most courageous, honorable, wise human beings I know.

Today I found myself back in bed by 11:00 – just lying there – feeling the cool breeze blowing across my face, smelling the briny scent coming off the bay – and I realized that I could just lie there all day and be perfectly content.

But eventually I roused myself, got up – figured I'd ride my bike to the post office and pick up the mail. Once I got to the post office I thought I'd go a little further – maybe stop in and see if Charles was at Tweets – I haven't seen him for a while and I was missing him. So I went on to Tweets – and Charles was there! Oh, it was so good to feel his smile coming through his Black Lives Matters mask! He said the exactly right words I needed – words that bolstered me up, inspired me, gave me hope. And then he told me my mocha was on him!

Sometimes all it takes is the kindness of a friend to make a day beautiful.

August 31, 2020

Today's gifts:

A cat nestled next to me on the chair - rubbing against my arm as I type; a nice walk on the boardwalk with Andrew and then vegan pizza at Ovn Pizza, sitting at a table that has both shade and sunshine - so with a little shift of our bodies we can warm up or cool off - and the wonderful Tracy Spring riding by on her bicycle and recognizing me even WITH my mask - and stopping to chat; the rest of my vegan pizza for dinner!; finding all kinds of wonderful memories as I dig and sort through more boxes; the office is almost functional now!; I slept through the night!; wonderful friends who lift me up with their love; a world full of talented, courageous, inspiring people who give me hope and help me know I'm not alone.

Andrew: Shall we meditate?
Karen: Yeah!

Another Four Years?

This morning's rant. I apologize in advance for any offense this may give, but…

IS THERE ANYONE WHO REALLY WANTS ANOTHER FOUR YEARS IN THIS COUNTRY LIKE THE LAST FOUR?!!! Holy crap. It's not just about what's happened since COVID-19 – it's all the other !@#$ leading up to COVID-19: Environmental protections squashed; the planet, literally, on fire; the seas rising, along with the deficit; big corporations and the CEOs who run them getting subsidized, while the poor keep getting poorer; the rise of hate crimes and racism (and all other brands of hate-ism); NAZI flags and Confederate battle flags in our streets; elections tampered with by a foreign power; long-time alliances lost; treaties ended; foreign service employees and the FBI under attack by our/their own president.

And last week this happened: Our president ordered police officers to tear gas peaceful protesters and clergy so that he could stand in front of a church, holding the Bible, for a photo opportunity.

Is anybody really enjoying the path our country is currently on?!!!

A.D.W. writes*: Since you asked? Yes! Four more years of campaign promises kept. Now… let the name calling begin.*

Karen writes*: I admire your courage for coming on here and speaking what feels true to you. Not going to call you any* *names or insult your or anything. I disagree with you - but that doesn't mean I don't like you or care about your well-being.*

Rather than calling each other names, do you think we might have a dialogue here - see if we can learn from each other maybe? Can you tell me, specifically, what campaign promises you are glad Mr. Trump made and kept?

***A.D.W. writes**: Oh. I can list them by heart. Most meaningful was -*

1. Moving the US Embassy to Jerusalem (many presidents promised but Trump DID it).

2. Allowing a one-time tax abatement to bring US companies back from overseas.

3. Forcing NATO signatories to pay the appropriate amount based on the individual nation's GNP, instead of the US filling the gap financially.

4. Increasing financial support for the legacy black colleges like Howard.

5. Expanding Enterprise Zones into more urban areas so that small businesses, including minority owned, can have reduced federal taxes as the zone gets to develop.

6. China! For years we all talked about the unfair trade situation.

7. Veterans. Revised rules so that bad doctors and administrators in VA hospitals could be fired!

8. *Medically. Allowed patients without hope to obtain experimental medications without being part of the test group.*

9. *Still advocates for schools of choice and charter and home schools; vouchers too! So that urban kids in failing schools can escape public school failures. If that's YOUR kid? It matters.*

10. *Border and immigration. Changing rules so that LEGAL immigration is the focus. Including showing the ability to be self-sustaining.*

11. *The wall.*

Karen writes: *Thank you for sharing the things that are important to you and that you value.*

Here's what I value and what's important to me - I value honesty, kindness and fairness.

As a recently-retired teacher who worked the last seven years of my career with a mostly Latinex population in a non-profit school, I'm going to focus on #9 and #10 of your list.

#9 Education. Our president created a fake university, Trump University, to collect tuition from unsuspecting students who just wanted to improve their lives. He was taken to court and had to pay a $25 million settlement. This does not show the workings of someone who values education. His son has called teachers "losers" - this does not show a man who was raised by his father to value the hard work of teachers.

#10 Immigrants. You put the emphasis on "legal" immigration. Is it legal to cross the U.S. border to seek asylum? Yup.

Many of my students have stories to tell about their journey to the United States through the border. They and their families were desperate to escape violence, oppression and poverty - and were willing to leave everything behind and risk their lives in the hope of making better lives for themselves here.

To see desperate people struggling to come to our land - as refugees protected by law - and then to see parents separated from children and to see them locked in cages - this is heart-breaking. It's inhumane. How any mother's heart can look at those scenes and not break is beyond my understanding.

And the wall that our president has been so eager to build? It has destroyed environmentally-protected land, encroached on the land of US citizens, and has not proven very effective. It has also taken money away from our military.

A.D.W. writes*: I taught a day in a Detroit school about architecture and urban planning and found it exhausting! I know it's hard work to do well!*

At some point you all have to explain why you'd support a party that will nominate someone like Hillary Clinton or Joe Biden.

Karen writes*: I don't really support parties or people so much as I support ideas (I didn't vote for Bill Clinton the second time he ran - I voted for Ralph Nader because I really liked his ideas). Neither Hillary Clinton nor Joe Biden were my first choices. But if I have to choose between a candidate who brags that he "grabs pussy," creates a fake university to bilk college students, takes money from his charities to fund his campaign (and is ordered to pay back $2 million by a judge), refuses to* *show his tax returns, and calls white supremacists "fine people" - and another candidate whose main problem is that he or she fails to inspire me - I will choose the uninspiring candidate over the criminal.*

And I guess I have to ask how you could still support Mr. Trump after he had peaceful protesters and clergy members tear gassed so he could have a photo op in front of the church in Washington, DC - do you not have a problem with that?

Kathy R.: *I think apathy and cynicism are pervasive and understandable. A certain percentage of people are always going to refuse to rethink things... but we have a generation who has tuned out. Some are now paying attention. I know I sound like an optimist. Sorry. It's tattered, but it is part of my fabric.*

Karen writes: *I have always loved your fabric, Kathy.*

Allen N. writes: *I have no objection to Trump building a Wall. I'll even lend him a trowel if he doesn't have one. Anything to keep him out of the White House!*

Jolyne writes: *Hi Karen!*

I've had this post in the back of my mind since I read it. I'm not going to pretend that I am a political person, because I'm not. I work 40+ hours a week in a stressful job. I am tired & all I want to do in my time off is relax. I say that because I get tired of all the retirees & other SAH people yelling, "Educate yourself!" I don't have the time or the energy to first figure out which news sources are even reliable, & then do the research.

That being said, I always watch the presidential debates. That is usually how I make my choice. I consider myself to be a conservative independent (I don't vote by party, but I do have conservative values). I knew Mr. Trump was a narcissistic ass back when I was watching him on Celebrity Apprentice. I HATED how he asked people questions, but then cut them off when they tried to answer. The thing is, I hated the Clintons more, so I voted for the Don.

Here is my current conundrum: Biden has dementia. It is unfathomable to me that the people of this country would vote a dementia sufferer to be our leader. In his current state, Biden doesn't have the mental capacity to organize a parade, much less run a country. His condition is obvious to anyone who has had the unfortunate experience of dealing with this disease. It is, & has been, obvious to the leaders of the Democratic party well before they chose him to be their nominee. So I can't help but ask why. What is the Democratic party up to? Who do they have up their sleeve? Who is a vote for Biden really going to? Not him. He might be the face, but who would be pulling the strings? Why is the Democratic party hiding that person from us? Their motives here are shady AT BEST. I just can't vote for a party that trusts the American people so little that they think they can pull some garbage like this & get away with it.

So to answer your question, I wish there were two different candidates representing the main parties come November. Since we are stuck with these two, I feel my only choice is to vote for Trump.

Karen writes:- *What an articulate post! I can totally hear your voice as I read this. And I feel your frustration. Believe me I do. I wish that BOTH of the major parties had honorable* *intelligent, honest people as their nominees for president. Wouldn't it be cool to actually have to choose between two people we admire and respect?*

But here we are.

My beloved father was dealing with a form of dementia in the last few years of his 101 years on this planet. Even with dementia he was one of the most intelligent, wise, perceptive people I knew. His memory wasn't so great - and sometimes he thought he was some place he wasn't - but his values never changed - he recognized decency when he saw it. He also recognized when someone wasn't being honest with him. He was pretty discerning of people. (He did not care for Mr. Trump.)

Even though I have experience with dementia in my family, I can't say that I'm fit to judge whether Biden has dementia or not (I know he has a stutter - and maybe people mistake that for dementia). I can say that he wasn't my first choice or even second, third, or fourth choice to be the nominee. I liked Elizabeth Warren a lot. I liked Bernie (I was a huge Bernie supporter in 2016). I liked Pete Boot-edge-edge. And yeah, I've sometimes questioned myself what is going on with the Democratic party. After the 2016 fiasco, I don't know that I'll ever entirely trust the Democratic leadership.

BUT I cannot abide having a bigot representing our country. Bigotry is a deal breaker for me.

Add on top of that all the other stuff: Bragging about "grabbing pussy"; starting a fake university to collect tuition from students hoping to make better lives for themselves;

having peaceful protesters and clergy people tear gassed so he can stand in front of a church holding a Bible; refusing to reveal his tax returns; destroying environmental regulations; building a wall on private land and destroying fragile ecosystems; refusing to pay his workers; and on and on. I will not vote for this man.

You wrote in your last sentence: "Since we are stuck with these two, I feel my only choice is to vote for Trump." I would say - since we are stuck with these two, I feel my only choice is to vote for Biden

Jeff Chase writes*: Our country faces the biggest test of my lifetime, and it's not the election. It's what comes after. Keep the faith and keep spreading love. People are growing.*

September

President Trump on Wednesday suggested that he might not accept the election results if he is not declared the winner in November, in response to a reporter's question about whether he would commit to a peaceful transfer of power — regardless of the outcome of the election.

"We're going to have to see what happens. You know that. I've been complaining very strongly about the ballots. And the ballots are a disaster," Trump said, alluding to his unsubstantiated arguments about widespread mail-in ballot fraud.

"Get rid of the ballots and you'll have a very peaceful — there won't be a transfer, frankly, there'll be a continuation..."

-Wise, Alana. "Trump Declines to Promise Peaceful Transition of Power After Election." NPR, 23 September, 2020. (https://www.npr.org/2020/09/23/916221894/trump-says-he-expect-election-results-to-end-up-at-supreme-court)

Shamelessly Happy

Today I gave myself permission to be shamelessly, incorrigibly happy - without excuse or guilt. It was GREAT!

Alrighty. Carry on then...

Allen N. writes*: The two of you are great: she who gave the permission to be happy, and she who ran gleefully with it.*

A Universe Alight

Rising above
the cacophony
lifted by Love
the noise wanes
as I gain
height until it ceases
to be and I am in flight
among the stars
a universe alight
with joy and hope
part of me, part of you,
we are part of this
every moment new
-Karen Molenaar Terrell

Middle of the Night

Middle of the night.
I get up to talk to
my Father-Mother.
She laughs with delight
opens her arms wide
and enfolds me in Love.
Home.
– Karen Molenaar Terrell

September 3, 2020

So Scotty and I take a walk on the boardwalk. When we get down to Boulevard Park, I'm thinking vegan pizza from Ovn, right? I make a call and order the pizzas – a couple to bring home to our vegan young people, too. Matt takes my order. I can tell right away – from our quick banter and the smile in his voice – that he has a sense of humor. I can have some fun here. We get to the part where I give him my credit card info and now he wants to know my name.

Karen: Okay, so my name is… don't laugh… my name is Karen.

Matt: (Laughing.)

Karen: (Laughing.) You're laughing.

Matt: (Continues laughing.) I'm only laughing because you told me not to laugh. But you sound like a very nice Karen.

Karen: (Still laughing.) Thank you.

Matt tells me that the pizza should be ready in 20 minutes – which is just about right for our walk back up from Boulevard Park.

When we get up to Ovn I give a call to let them know we've arrived. When Matt picks up the phone I feel myself instantly smiling – I'm so glad it's him! He knows how to laugh.

Karen: This is Karen. We're here now. Hey – do you have any truffle salt?

Matt: No, unfortunately we don't have any right now – we can't import it because of COVID.

Karen: Bummer. Do you have any other cool stuff there?

Matt: (Laughing.) We have all kinds of cool stuff here. We've got smoked salt and habanero salt. We've got... (and he lists a whole bunch of other salts – but my mind has wrapped itself around habanero salt – that sounds pretty interesting.)

Karen: Habanero salt – does that have any animal products in it?

Matt: No animal products. It's really spicey, though.

Karen: Spicey! Cool! We'll take a habanero salt and a smoked salt, too.

Matt: You got it!

Karen: Thank you!

Pretty soon Matt comes out with the pizzas. I finally get to see my new friend! Of course, we're both wearing masks – but I can still tell he's smiling under there.

Matt: Are you Karen?

Karen: Yes – are you Matt?

Matt: (Smiling.) Yes. Here are your pizzas. (Hands me the stack of pizzas.) Thank you for giving Karens such a good name.

Karen: Thank you so much! It was nice meeting you!

Andrew and I were sitting at a picnic table at Boulevard Park last week - just chatting and watching the doings around us - when suddenly this little acorn plopped down from the sky and landed on the table between us. We both started laughing - it was like this little fellow did not want to be ignored - "Here I am! Here I am!" So I brought him home and today I planted him in a pot. We'll see what happens...

I Think We're Good to Go

Mask? Check.
Teeth brushed? Check.
Hair combed? Check.
Shirt without food on it? Check.
I think we're good to go.
– Karen Molenaar Terrell

September 5, 2020

My dear Humoristian hooligans –

I apologize that I haven't sent you any messages lately. I'm afraid I haven't been feeling very humoristic. It is a sad truth that sometimes the world needs more than Groucho glasses and whoopee cushions to make everything better.

But when I think of you – my Humoristian friends – out there on the planet, working your magic – it brings me hope. May your indefatigable good will touch the lost and frightened and alone. May your irrepressible joy bring hope to the discouraged and desolate. May your unflappable kindness transform the stingy, stodgy and stuffy. May the bigots and bullies be overcome by your steadfast, unshakable love for your fellow creatures. May you bring courage to the ascared.

You are making a difference.
Karen

Those of you who are familiar with my drives with my centenarian father might remember that our go-to place for Dad's root beer floats was Sisters Espresso, and that my drink of choice was usually a lavender green iced tea.

Sisters Espresso is assuming new ownership in a week and my husband and I wanted to stop by and order some of our last drinks from our friends, the current owners. Brooke was behind the window and I felt a little tug of nostalgia when I saw her back there, working her magic at the espresso machine. She looked up and smiled when she saw me, and pointed to her special for the day: "The Karen" – a lavender green tea! And she named it for me - not the Karen meme!

I have never had a drink named after me before! And to see the name "Karen" used in a happy way almost brought tears to my eyes.

Of course, I had to order one of those Karen specials for myself. (It was on the house.)

In a Bubble in the Fog

In a peaceful bubble inside the fog
I sit on a picnic bench, sipping my mocha,
and watch the mother playing with her toddlers
on the beach – constructing buildings of sand
and a woman is lifting her kayak onto her car
"Can I help?" I ask. She laughs behind her mask
and shakes her head no – she has done this
many times before – but thank you for the offer!
For a little while I take a break from what lies
on the other side of the grounded clouds.
Without being able to give you the reasons why
I know I am safe in this bubble in the fog.
– Karen Molenaar Terrell

September 9, 2020

Xander joined me today for my annual Table Mountain hike. It was amazing up there! I really needed this - really needed to get back up in the mountains and ozone again. For a little while we were able to forget the pandemic, and the division, and the political insanity going on "down below" and escape to a place that exists outside all of that. We were hugged in the arms of Mount Baker - surrounded by alpine butterflies and purple fireweed blooming out of craggly rocks - with Mount Shuksan rising rocky-ridged and glacier-robed behind us.

It was a perfect day.

A Boa Constrictor House

We have a boa constrictor house
big lumps of boxes and books and sacks
pass through and fill closets and shelves,
nooks and crannies, corners and cracks –
before what's left empties into "free" piles –
parents' and sons' and our life's culls
expanding and shrinking the belly
of the beast – full, then purged, then full
again – in a never-ending cycle of recycling.
– Karen Molenaar Terrell

September 13, 2020

You may remember the story about the intrepid little sunflower who was sawed in half by a slug earlier in the summer and grew new roots in a bottle. I transplanted her to a pot and put her out on the side of the house by her sister – where she'd originally been when she was attacked in the infamous Slug Wars. She thrived and grew out there and now she's blooming!

Because she's in a pot I was able to move her away from the dark background of the house for a photo of her in the sunlight. Look at her! All growed-up!

***

Warning: Highly-organized individuals may find these images disturbing.

Scott and I have combined our offices to free up another room. And... here's my desk area. I don't even know what to say. I'm simultaneously shaking my head in embarrassment and smiling with happy memories

September 16, 2020

See? This is why we shouldn't put business executives in charge of our schools, prisons, courts, military, environment, or nation. Business executives think in terms of financial profit, rather than social progress; competition, rather than cooperation; what we can do for THEM, rather than what they can do for US. They aren't going to go out of their way to help you if your home is burning, your family is sick, you're being attacked by racists – unless there's some way for their company to gain something from it. A CEO's goal is to beat out and squash the competition (anyone who doesn't work for their financial company) and win the race for the most wealth accumulated. Their goal is to prepare students to serve them in their corporations. Their goal is to privatize prisons, health care, schools, parks, and the postal service to make a profit. Their instinct is to use the natural environment for short-term financial gain, rather than to conserve and preserve it for future generations.

Are business executives "bad" people? Nope. But if they want to work as public servants, they can no longer be business executives – they need to give up their positions, wealth, and instincts as business people and shift their perspective – look at the world in a whole new way – because business and politics don't mix.

A Poem-Prayer

A morning poem-prayer for the world:

There is no spot where Love is not.
There is no spot where Truth is not.
There is no spot where Life is not.

Love fills all space –
we can never be separated from Love –
there's no place where we don't feel
Love's presence, enveloping us in peace
and pure tender kindnesses that heal
us – bringing sweet renewal like the gentle
rains and the morning dew upon the grass.
In dauntless joyful humility we kneel
to give thanks. To praise. To serve.

Love's presence is all-powerful.
NOTHING has the power to usurp
Love's governing of Her own creation.
We are the manifestations, expressions, reflections,
ideas, children of Love – made in Her likeness.
All we can feel is what Love feels.
All we can know is what Truth knows.
All we can be is what Love made us to be.
We exist by Love and for Love and with Love.
"For Love alone is Life"

Fear, hatred, greed, condemnation,
and self-righteous indignation
have no place in Love's creation.
Give them no power. Pay them no heed.
Let Love be our guide; Let Love lead.
-Karen Molenaar Terrell

Joy Without Reason

My joy is not dependent on matter –
not dependent on flattering chatter –
my clothes can be in tatters,
my ego-dreams all shattered,
and possessions scattered –
but I'm alive! I can love! I can learn!
Joy is not something I have to earn –
not something I need a reason
or a special season
to feel.
– Karen Molenaar Terrell

September 17, 2020

Here's what I need tonight – I need to remind myself that we can't always see how things will work themselves out – and sometimes salvation comes in completely unexpected ways. I need to remind myself of the amazing things that I've witnessed and experienced in the last several years during times when I saw no solution and things looked pretty bleak.

Back in February 2017 I found myself in a position that seemed impossible. Mom was in the hospital with congestive heart failure and Dad soon followed her there with a UTI. They were on two different floors, both struggling to stay alive. I'd visit one and then the other – and then go home, on high alert, waiting for the phone to ring and for someone to drop some new crisis onto me.

Just two days before Mom was going to be released from the hospital into hospice care, a hospital social worker told me that it looked like the assisted living care facility wasn't going to accept Mom back into her and Dad's home because of her medical issues. I told the social worker that the assisted living place hadn't told me anything about this, and surely they would have let me know, right? But she seemed pretty sure about this. So I called the assisted living place on Saturday and was told that Mom was going to be evaluated on Monday morning to determine if she could be brought back to her home. Which. Hospice needed to set things up for her – and they needed to know right then where they should send the equipment. I needed answers immediately. Finally, the assisted living lady told me (under her breath) that if she was me she'd be looking for another place for my mother and father.

I had two days to find a new home for my parents.

In a panic, I started calling other assisted living places and soon realized that the cost of the care my parents were going to need in the facilities would clean out their savings in a couple months. I thought maybe I could use my retirement savings to help them – but that wouldn't last too long, either. And – honestly, I didn't want to send my parents to some strange, unfamiliar place that looked like an institution. The thought came to me, then, that I should bring Mom and Dad into my home when they were released from the hospital, and provide the care myself. Scotty agreed to this plan and agreed to help. (I married an incredible man.)

I was still teaching full-time then – so this was going to be tricky.

But I told the social workers at the hospital that I wanted Mom brought to my home when she was released on Monday. She asked me if I was sure – I think she was concerned about me – but I told her yes. It felt right. Hospice got in touch with me – bless them! – and, when Mom was brought by ambulance to our home, a hospice nurse came over and showed Scott and I how to care for her.

I'm so very glad Love guided me to make this decision for Moz. I'm so glad she was brought to our home, surrounded by our love. We spent the whole day telling each other how much we loved each other – and in the wee hours of the morning, while I dozed on the couch next to her hospital bed, she passed.

I felt myself brushed by joy and peace and love, and woke to find she was gone.

So now I had to find a home for Dad – I'd promised Moz that she didn't need to worry about him – that we'd make sure he was alright. Originally the plan had been to bring him into our home where he could be with Mom, but now that she was gone our home wouldn't be the right place for him. He needed the kind of care that someone with skills greater than my own could give him. The social worker asked us if we'd ever looked into adult family homes, and gave us a booklet with names and phone numbers.

When I got home from the hospital after my visit with Dad and the social worker, I went for a walk – at this point I was completely emotionally and mentally stretched – feeling out of my depth and scared about the future – and I needed to find some peace for myself. And suddenly a rainbow arched across the sky – and it felt like a promise! – like Moz was there with me, reassuring me, telling me everything was going to be alright. I began making phone calls to adult family homes – and on the second call I felt I'd found the right place. My brother and I went over to check it out – there were bird feeders in the front yard, and cats and dogs – and I knew the woman who answered the door would have been someone Moz would have felt an instant kinship with. AND the cost of care for Dad would fit his budget!

I felt like a weight was lifted from my shoulders. We had found Dad's new home – a place I didn't even know existed a day before!

We just never know.

NOTHING is impossible to Love. NOTHING.

The intrepid little sunflower is hosting a party on her petals today - she is alive with bees. It's cool to think of her being part of honey someday.

September 18, 2020

More proof of Love's care: The Year of Insanity.

Thirteen years ago I went insane. I did not like it so much. But I learned a lot from it. It occurs to me now that the experience I had during The Year of Insanity helped prepare me for the challenges our world is facing right now.

I believe mankind is experiencing a collective insanity today. And recognizing that is what is going on is giving me some compassion for my world and its inhabitants. I understand what this feels like. I understand that shaming someone who is mentally ill is not going to make things better. Laying guilt on someone going through a massive clinical depression - as I went through - is not going to heal that individual, or the world. Hating someone who is not herself or himself or their self, and is already contemplating suicide, is not going to fix the problem.

Having personally experienced mental illness I know the one and only thing that can reach through the fog of insanity and heal mental illness is love.

We need to recognize that those individuals who are experiencing and exhibiting mental illness right now are not themselves. This isn't THEM. Their real identity - OUR real identity - is secure and safe - "hid with Christ" in Love - where goodness and purity and intelligence and wisdom and kindness and honesty are eternally, indestructibly qualities of who we ALL really are.

Thirteen years ago I wasn't sure I was going to make it to today - I contemplated suicide daily. But look at all I would have missed if I'd given up on life then! - All the beautiful new friends I wouldn't have met! The sunsets and sunrises I wouldn't have seen! The lessons I wouldn't have learned! The changes I wouldn't have been able to make! The love and laughter I would have denied myself!

When I was deep in the depression I couldn't imagine a happy ending to my story. I couldn't imagine I'd ever get out of it. Couldn't imagine it ever ending.

But then one day the fog lifted and I awakened from the nightmare. I looked out on the world and I was connected again - connected to the joy and the beauty and a sense of well-being. I had myself back again.

Now I'm really grateful for that year of learning - that year of shedding the chrysalis (and that feels like what the whole world is doing right now). I learned a new appreciation for the power of Love; gained a new appreciation for the power of a moment and a good, deep breath; I came to appreciate the power of choice; and gained renewed gratitude for all the beauty in Nature and mankind; I gained greater humility, empathy, and compassion for others; and a stronger commitment to my own spiritual journey.

I learned I can be happy even when I'm sad.

"There's nothing in a caterpillar that tells you it's going to be a butterfly."
- Richard Buckminster Fuller

"The very circumstance, which your suffering sense deems wrathful and afflictive, Love can make an angel entertained unawares."
- Mary Baker Eddy

The RBG Rap

Her name was Ruth
and she stood for Truth
She worked for justice -
the rights of all of us
She was fearless, peerless
a woman of honor
no one on earth
could ever con her
When I grow up I want to be
just like the mighty RBG
- Karen Molenaar Terrell

September 21, 2020

I so love my walks in Bellingham! I always meet such
wonderful people (and dogs) on my walks!

Today I was walking along the sidewalk that's next to the
parking area in Boulevard Park and I tripped over a bump, felt
my ankle start to turn, started to go down, and then quickly
caught my balance and righted myself. I started laughing at
myself under my mask - I crack myself up - and then I noticed
two young women sitting in a car facing me. I could tell they
weren't sure how to respond - they looked like they wanted to
laugh, but didn't want to be rude. I pointed at them, grinning - I
know they could see the smile in my eyes: "Did you see that?"
I asked. They nodded their heads and started laughing with me.
"But I made a good recovery, didn't I?" And they nodded their
heads in agreement.

One of them yelled through the window - "That was a GREAT
recovery!"

"Yes. Thank you! Thank you!" I said in my best Elvis Presley
imitation and moved on. It's so fun to find people who can
laugh with you.

Just before I left the park to begin my walk back, I got out my
cellphone and ordered vegan pizzas from the Ovn pizza place
to bring back to the family. I've ordered pizzas from them
before and know the routine now. When the pizza guy got to
the part where he asked for my name, I said, "Don't laugh. My
name is Karen."

He said, "Oh! You've ordered here before from Matt, haven't you?"

I affirmed this.

He said, "Matt says you are just delightful!"

And that totally made my day.

September 25, 2020

I woke up smiling this morning - just full of hope and happiness. I was having a dream - I can't remember the specifics of it now - but the sons were in it, and Scotty, and my friends, Jamie and Kathi - and we were celebrating something wonderful together.

Isn't it amazing the power in a full night's sleep and happy dreams?

I woke up knowing everything is alright, and is going to BE alright.

To the dear anonymous someone who gifted me with a $20 credit at Sisters Espresso -

Thank you! Your kind gesture meant so much to me! I have no idea who you are - I don't know your religion, gender, politics, or age - and I LOVE that! You could be any of us - your kindness represents the best in all of us - and I'm not sure I can find the words to convey how much I needed to see that right now.

Bless you!
Karen

Response to a Friend Who Tagged Me in a Post

I'm guessing that any dialogue we have about this is just going to be frustrating and futile for both of us. I love you - but I do not agree with your assessment of Mr. Trump's abilities to lead this country. If you're really interested, here is my response -

Yes, I'm glad Trump used 35 million in Justice Department grants to help aid human trafficking victims - but I think we need to be clear that this wasn't his personal money - this was actually OUR money - as tax payers - that he used for this. (As we don't know if Trump has ever paid taxes because he refuses to show us his tax returns - it might be assumed that he, personally, contributed NOTHING to helping these victims.) You mentioned Bill Clinton - I did not vote for Bill Clinton the second time he ran for president because he struck me as dishonest (I voted for Ralph Nader). Trump has shown me he is dishonest, also - time and again his actions and words have proven this.

Mr. Trump could care less about protecting women – he is himself a sex predator. He has bragged about entering the rooms of teenage beauty contestants as they dress. He has bragged about "grabbing pussy." He has been accused of rape and sexual harassment by dozens of women - and no, there is no excuse for any of this. I wonder if all those who shrug Trump's behavior off as "locker room" antics would be shrugging it off if Mr. Trump were Black. If a Black man had bragged about "grabbing pussy" and entering the rooms of teenage beauty contestants – if a Black man had been accused of sexual harassment by dozens of women - would it be shrugged off?

How anyone who is against sex trafficking can support Mr. Trump is beyond my understanding. Mr. Trump is not an honorable man. If he has some secret to ending sex trafficking then he should have let us all know about it long ago so the sex trafficking would end. You have been totally focused on this one thing - sex trafficking - for months now. And sex trafficking is evil - of course! - but what about the children separated from their mothers and still locked in cages?! What about Mr. Trump's mocking of the disabled?! What about the disrespect he's shown to our veterans?! What about the money he stole from his charity to use for himself?! What about the way he sent in military police to push aside peaceful protesters so he could hold a Bible in front of a church that didn't want him there?!

Mr. Trump is not worthy to lead this nation.

Dawn B. writes: *Nailed it!*

Sheila K. writes: *Silence is violence - glad you posted.*

Jessie N. writes: *Bravo, Karen. Standing ovation BRAVO.*

A.D.W. writes: *Locker room talk. His actions speak louder than words. Of course, it's the taxpayer's money. As to taxes, he has repeatedly said that as soon as the review is complete he'll share them (as a complicated business his taxes are in multiple binders) - although he has no requirement to do so.*

Jim S. writes*: What I find truly fascinating about our time is that I could write something like:*

"This is the most important election of the last 150 years, if not maybe in the entire existence of the country. Never has evil been so prevalent and brazen. Never have our liberties been more threatened. Never have we been at such a tipping point where the end of America as an entity is a real possibility."

And both sides would fervently agree.

October

For October, 3,033 fires (8th least since 2000) burned 1,020,326 acres (most on record), which is 336.4 acres burned/fire (most on record). For January - October, 47,194 fires (4th least since 2000) burned 8,545,166 acres (6th most on record), which is 181.1 acres burned/fire (most on record).

- NOAA, October 2020.
(https://www.ncdc.noaa.gov/sotc/fire/202010)

The Olden Days

Remember the olden days when we just walked into stores and cafes like we belonged there? Good times. Good times.

Alrighty. Carry on then...

October 1, 2020

A Friend: Karen, did you watch the debate?

Karen: Every painful minute of it.

A Friend: What did you think?

Karen: "Stand back and stand by"?!! If 40% of my fellow citizens are fine with that then we are in real trouble here.

A Friend: No, he just misspoke.

Karen: If he misspoke then he needs to clarify that. He needs to very clearly say, "I denounce the Proud Boys. I denounce white supremacists. White supremacy has no place in our nation." And he needs to say this without having his fingers crossed behind his back and without a wink-wink nudge-nudge. He has had two days now to denounce the Proud Boys and he has not done this. I think we can assume he's not going to.

A Friend: But did you notice Biden didn't answer any questions?

Karen: Right. Did you notice that the other candidate didn't give him a chance to?

A Friend: Well, Biden should be able to handle that kind of pressure if he's going to be president.

Karen: Biden is not a preschool teacher. He shouldn't be expected to placate toddlers. Presidents move on the world stage – dealing with other international leaders who are grown-ups – dealing with preschoolers is not Biden's area of expertise, and we shouldn't expect it to be.

(I wish I'd taken a photo of the faces of the PBS commentators at the end of the debate to paste here. They looked like they'd

just been through a battle – eyes wide, faces drawn. I felt
tremendous sympathy for them and empathy with them.)

October 2, 2020

There have been several times in my life when I have had the opportunity to learn more of who I am by being put in a position where I needed to respond to violence, or the threat of violence.

– Once I was waiting to pick up my son from a movie and I saw a young man sitting on top of another young man, pounding his head into the parking lot pavement. Without thinking, I walked into the ring of young spectators watching this happen, and tried to pull the attacker off his victim. I yelled, "Stop it! You're killing him!" And one of the spectators said, "Lady, you better be careful. This guy could have a knife!"

I turned on him and asked him why he was just watching - why he wasn't trying to help. And then I put my hands on my hips and announced, "I AM A TEACHER!" – like I was some kind of super hero or something and that was going to make them all stop. The guy who was smashing the other guy's head into the pavement sort of paused then, and looked up at me for a minute, and then went back to doing what he was doing.

There were other people there – outside the circle, watching while this was happening – but at one point I remember looking up to see another parent – the mother of one of my son's friends – had stepped into the circle with me. I remember being amazed by this and she said, "Well, I wasn't going to let you be in here alone!" That's always stayed with me – that this woman I didn't know well had stepped into the circle with me to back me up.

Pretty soon the police came out and took care of it all.

Afterwards I realized what I'd done was pretty foolish – but I was glad I'd done it anyway. I'd learned something about myself that night.

– I remember feeling some fear as I drove to participate in the local BLM rally last June – there'd already been some stories of guys with pistols and rifles showing up at other rallies to intimidate the protesters and I'd heard rumors that there'd be some of these guys at this rally, too. But I remember coming to terms with that as I drove there – praying for the safety of EVERYone there – protesters and gun folks alike. When I pulled into the parking lot, sure enough, there were guys with rifles slung over their shoulders and holsters with guns and assorted other black metal things tucked away in belts and pockets. I got out of the car, pulled on my mask, and made eye contact with a man with a rifle – raised my eyebrows and pointed to my "TRUTH JUSTICE KINDNESS" sign – and I remember he kind of smiled and said, "We hope so." And in that moment – maybe when I realized these guys with the weapons were the ones who were really scared – all fear just vanished for me. The rally was a peaceful one.

– And this is a story I haven't shared until now, but I think now is the right time. One time when I was working at a nonprofit school another teacher came out of her office – still talking to the student that was in her office as she approached me – and handed me the note you see below: "We are not SAFE." I'm going to skip everything that happened after this, except for this one part: At one point I had a clear choice – one choice brought sure safety for myself, but left my colleague on her own (this is the choice I know my colleague wanted me to make for myself) – and the other choice brought possible danger to myself, but meant I would stay by my colleague through this experience. I took a deep breath and chose to stay with my friend. I'm so grateful I made that choice. I don't know how I'd live with myself if I hadn't.

And I'm happy to say that's what it all comes down to for me now – I'm no longer so concerned about how other people feel about me – these days I'm more concerned with how I feel about myself. I know I won't always make the "right choice" – I still mess up majorly sometimes – but I'm learning more and more I can trust myself – and there is a certain power in that, you know?

October 3, 2020

The privilege to be kind belongs to everyone and can't be taken away.

I wish no one ill.

My dear Humoristian hooligans –

2020 has been a crazy ride, hasn't it? Dad died on January 19th and two days later the first case of COVID was reported in our state (and the country). Dad had good timing. 2020 has brought COVID-19, murder hornets, wildfires, hurricanes, tornadoes, plagues, pestilence, political insanity, and every emotion a person can possibly feel – grief, terror, anger, fear, and also immense love, gratitude, and, (especially lately) hope.

And, sitting here, I just realized I'm not "ascared" anymore. At some point – maybe when the craziness reached epic and absurd proportions – the fear just dissolved. It was like – okay, what else you got? Bring it on, baby! I think it's going to be hard to ever again scare anyone who's survived 2020. (I just had a flashback of one of my favorite cartoons – a lady with a bun on top of her head, whistling in hell – and one of the devil's helpers saying to him: "We can't scare her - she was a middle school teacher." As a former middle school teacher that one always cracked me up. I think that same cartoon could have the caption: "You can't scare her - she survived 2020" and it would still work.)

Keep working your magic, my friends! Keep shining your light! The world has need of your pluck and courage and unfailing kindness!

– Karen

Limerick for a Little Fly

There once was an adventurous fly
who journeyed from his home in the sty
he followed the bright lights
to the stage in the heights
and became famous that night by and by.
– Karen Molenaar Terrell

October 8, 2020

I put my mom's CD into my car's voice box a few days ago and Moz has been singing to me on my drives. I've felt her loving presence with me a lot lately - not as a ghost or anything - but just as... well, as Moz.

October 11, 2020

My husband and I came back to Mount Rainier this weekend. We rented the Jimmy Beech House – the same house where my dad, Dee Molenaar, celebrated his 100th birthday two years ago. It felt good to be back. I remembered Dad surrounded by his old mountaineering friends and his family as they celebrated him. He sat in that chair and slept in that bed. And he laughed and reminisced and stuck his finger in the icing of his cake right over there.

It rained on us this weekend – buckets of wet fell from the sky and dumped on us – it was GREAT! While we were inside we drank tea and watched movies and The Seahawks and sat in front of the fire in the fireplace – it was very cozy. But we also went hiking, of course, because… well, that's what hikers do, right? We drove up to Paradise on Saturday and did a quick hike up to Alta Vista to say hi to Mom and Dad's ashes. It stopped raining for a bit and we watched the clouds drift by in the valley below us. When we got back down to Paradise it started snowing – great gusts of snow blowing in our faces and whipping around us – the first snowfall of the season there. We'd started a second hike, but turned around at Myrtle Falls because of the weather.

Today we drove back up to the park, but only went as far as Longmire this time. (When we entered the park we were told by the ranger lady that there was a lot of snow at Paradise now and traction tires were recommended. I'm glad we got up there yesterday.) So we did a quick easy hike on the Trail of

Shadows loop and then hiked a bit up the Wonderland Trail towards Cougar Rock Campground.

I told my husband about a hike I remembered doing years ago in my twenties – Eagle Peak – and thought maybe that was something we could do while we were at Longmire – I remembered it as fairly easy. But when we checked it out we saw it was labeled "strenuous" and was more than seven miles long with an elevation gain of 3,000 feet. Which. What the heck?! I started sort of chuckling then, remembering my strong young self – and the adventures I used to have – going off by myself for a "quick hike" of some peak. I'm so glad I had those adventures! And I'm also really glad I survived them.

I didn't mention my dad to strangers all weekend. This is kind of a big deal for me. Normally I find every opportunity to let people know I'm the daughter of a famous mountaineer and I used to work at Rainier and… and… did I mention I've climbed to the summit? But this weekend I kept all that a secret. I asked other people for directions. I played the part of the tourist. And it felt really good.

Even on the Challenging Days

You know what? Even on the challenging days –
the should-have-stayed-in-bed days –
there is still Love.
there is still Truth.
there is still Good.
Nothing can separate us from what really matters –
not lost phones, nor spilled juice, nor forgotten passwords.
When it all shakes down, when the breakable shatters,
still there is Love.-
Karen Molenaar Terrell

October 16, 2020

Registered Democrat here. A few things –
1) I've never collected welfare.
2) I've never collected unemployment.
3) I've never been on Medicaid.
4) I've never had an abortion.
5) I've worked almost my entire adult life as a teacher.

More things:
1) Although I've never needed welfare, unemployment compensation, or Medicaid – I've never begrudged these things to the people who DO need them. I don't mind contributing to a federal pot of money to help my fellow Americans who are in need. I consider that is one of the privileges and responsibilities of being a citizen of this country. It's not all about me. It's not "me first." Being a citizen of the United States is about being a part of something bigger than myself. It's about caring for the well-being of others in my country, too.

2) Although I've never had an abortion – was never in a position where that was something I needed to think about – I don't believe it's my place to make that choice for another woman. Being pregnant is a big deal. Childbirth is a big deal. Women die from these things. Medical decisions regarding a woman's health should be between the woman and her doctor – and are not anyone else's business. My pregnancies were planned and celebrated. I was healthy. My sons were healthy in the womb. We anticipated our sons' births with great excitement and joy. But I can imagine circumstances being

different. I have friends who had to make that choice – and I know it wasn't easy for any of them. NO ONE IS FOR ABORTION.

We Will Always Share This Bond

We've learned a lot about ourselves
in the last four years, haven't we?
We've learned what we're made of,
what needed to be fixed, what's
important to us, and what we love.
We came together, worked shoulder-
to-shoulder, side by side,
bolstering each other up,
sharing inspiration, sharing the ride,
sharing a good laugh now and then,
letting Love guide.
We're maybe not looking our best –
we're battle-weary, battered, bedraggled –
but we're not beaten.
And look at all we've done together!
We will always share this bond, my friend.
– Karen Molenaar Terrell

The Great Division of 2016-2020

Grandma, what did you do
during The Great Division?
Were you a part of the revision?
Were you a part of the decision
to follow a new vision
and heal the fission?
Did you walk in marches
and write letters?
Did you go to rallies
to make things better?
Did you do everything you could
to help the jobless and poor
the disenfranchised and mocked –
could you have done more?

Grandma, did you vote?
– Karen Molenaar Terrell

October 17, 2020

I have something to share – but I want to preface this by saying this is not a "I'm-so-cool" story – this is a… wow… when-people-learn-you-want-to-do-something-good-they-celebrate-that-and-want-to help story. This is a people-are-good story. This is a God-will-find-a-way-to-provide-for-Her-children story – and sometimes God will provide by using US. And when that happens – when we're the ones who are in the right place at the just right time – it is magic!!

So. I guess this story starts a week ago when I saw a homeless lady sitting near Tony's Coffee Shop with her shopping cart home. I asked her if I could get her a coffee or something, and she came with me to Tony's and I got her a scone and a mocha. She was/is very cool and I consider her a new friend. I ran into her again today – we were happy to see each other again! – and she asked if I could get her a sandwich for lunch. I said sure – I'd get her something after my walk.

After my walk I came back to my new friend and she introduced me to another homeless person – a young man my youngest son's age. The young man said he didn't need anything to eat, but – and he lifted up his foot to show me his shoe (the bottom of his shoe was hanging to the top by a few stitches – it was flapping around) what he really needed was a new pair of shoes. Then he wandered off – not expecting anything from me – and I went to get a sandwich for my friend and to get myself something to eat at the Colophon Cafe.

When I came out of the Colophon the young man was sitting next to my friend again. I asked him if he knew of any shoe stores near by – and he looked at me in shock – "Are you going to get me shoes?" he asked, with a mixture of uncertainty and hope. I told him yeah – he couldn't go walking around in those shoes he was wearing. So he got off the bench and we went on a quest for new shoes.

As he was walking his shoe kept flapping against the pavement and he joked that it was making music – it was like a drum. He asked me my name and I hesitated… because… you know… people with my name are sometimes hesitant to say it these days …but I told him "Karen" and waited for a reaction. He apparently hadn't heard about the Karen memes, though, and when I told him what "Karen" has come to mean, he laughed and said, "You are the least like that person that I know!"

He told me his name was Vlad – short for Vladimir – and he'd been born in Russia, but adopted when he was young by people in Minnesota. I asked him what he was doing out here and he said he really liked it here. We talked some more about his circumstances – and as I got to know him better I felt all my motherly instincts coming out.

After several stops, we finally found a place that sold men's shoes – "Fairhaven Runners" – and went in to investigate (everyone in my family has purchased shoes at Fairhaven Runners at some point). Vlad found some shoes that he really liked and the shoe salesclerk – who quickly grasped what was happening – patiently explained to Vlad how he could measure his feet for the shoe size and then went back to fetch some shoes for him to try on. As Vlad was trying on shoes, the salesclerk asked Vlad if he could use some free socks and Vlad looked up at him with a smile on his face and nodded his head. The salesclerk went in the back room and then came out and tossed Vlad some free new socks for Vlad to wear with his new shoes.

I told Vlad he could leave with his new shoes now and I would take care of everything for him in the store. Vladimir thanked me and went out smiling. There was a lady standing behind us in the store and she asked me, "Did you just buy him new shoes?!" She looked like she was crying. She said that it was really beautiful what she'd just witnessed. Isn't that lovely?!

And then – get this! – when the salesclerk rang me up he gave me a 20% discount! And THAT had ME tearing up. People WANT to do right by each other, don't they?

I felt like I was walking on holy ground today. I think… I think it all balances out, you know? – Good disperses itself throughout the cosmos – and I know I'll always have what I need – there's no lack – there's no competition – there's no need to go through life clutching and afraid and feeling like Good is limited and finite, and if someone else has enough then I won't have enough.

Sure, there have been times when I've been led to say "no" – times when I've felt that giving money to someone wasn't going to really help him – I'm not completely naive when it comes to stuff like that. But this time – today – I knew it was right. And it felt really good that I was there to be used by Love in this way.

Dodging Caterpillars

Empty country roads
I'm dodging caterpillars
Tiger moths in spring!
-Karen Molenaar Terrell

Gold Stripes in the Autumn

I love gold stripes
on the road in autumn
as my window wiper wipes
raindrops off my windshield
or the sun shines through
the leaves making them look
like stained glass set in a blue
sky .
– Karen Molenaar Terrell

October 22, 2020

Last night we went to Peace Arch Park on the Canadian border
and looked across the street to Canada. I watched crows and
seagulls brazenly flying back and forth across the border – to
the U.S. – to Canada – back to the U.S. – and there was
something about that that really tickled me. There was a young
trio of friends (originally from Congo, but here to go to school)
who'd never been to Canada before – they stood together on
the border and let us take their photo. Most all the lanes going
"into" and "out of" are closed now (ferme) and the gate under
the Peace Arch is closed while "progress" is made. (A
metaphor for 2020?) But we could see the Canadian flag
waving across the street, and a nice Canadian policeman waved
back to me from his side of the street and let me take his photo.

What is it about pumpkins? I was wandering through Gordon's
Pumpkin Farm today and I realized I was smiling under my
mask. Smiling at pumpkins. (!) They are a friendly vegetable,
aren't they?

Ode to Pumpkins

Shiny round-cheeked pumpkin
Nestled in my autumn garden
You may become a lantern.
You may become a pie.
You may become a hardy soup
on my stove top, by and by.
– Karen Molenaar Terrell

Limerick to a Pumpkin

There once was a punkin' named Jack
who appeared in the patch in the back.
He was orange and round
and grew up on a mound –
He was the star of Halloween –
that's a fact.
– Karen Molenaar Terrell

Pumpkin Haiku

Round friendly pumpkin
Waiting now for Halloween
Soon he'll be compost.
– Karen Molenaar Terrell

October 24, 2020

The trumpeter swans are back for the winter! I've been waiting for them - scanning the skies and fields for a sign of them - and, today, I finally had my first swan-sighting when a pair of them went winging over my head. I felt my spirits rise as soon as I saw them. As long as there is such beauty in the world, I know there is hope.

October 29, 2020

My dear Humoristian hooligans –

Only five more days. Whatever befalls, know that your humor and wit, courage and honesty, compassion and kindness, have mattered. You have made a difference in our world. None of the good you've done has been wasted. I am so grateful to know you – each and every radiant, rascally, raspberry-blowing rapscallion one of you.

The world needs you. May those weary wanderers athirst for a kind word in a desert of rudeness find comfort in your good-natured cheer. May the ascared and lonely find hope in the smiling eyes above your masks. May you bring laughter to those in desperate need of a healthy guffaw. May the bigots, bullies, braggarts, and busybodies be transformed by your irrepressible, irresistible joy and good will.

Polish your kazoos, bring out the whoopee cushions, don your Groucho glasses and your Lucy wigs – avail yourselves of every tool in your Humoristian bag of tricks – and go out there and work your magic!

Karen "Wingoof-Wingoov" Molenaar Terrell

If You Meant to Say

I think it might be helpful to us to be aware that those who identify as Democrats and those who identify as Republicans are being fed completely different narratives about the state of our country. (Check out the new movie on Netflix, "The Social Dilemma.") I just had an interesting conversation with a conservative friend, Jim S. – someone I have come to respect over the years because he doesn't get defensive, doesn't view me as "the enemy," is willing to listen to what I have to say, has the courage to share what he believes in an honest and forthright way, and is able to self-reflect. Jim knows how to question me, but he also knows how to question himself. I think this is a rare and beautiful thing.

Anyway. We were talking about Trump and white supremacy, Antifa and The Proud Boys and the Boogaloo movements. Throwing out different links and articles to each other. And it was hugely eye-opening to me! Jim S. is getting a completely different narrative than me!

I'm not going to share all the links and articles, stories and narratives – all of that is out there – available to any of us who are willing to cross the river and see what the other guy sees from where he's camped.

And, of course, our back-and-forthing didn't change in any way the different perspectives we have of the world – I still see things from my perspective (vote Biden!), and Jim still sees things from his perspective. But what the dialoguing DID do for me is help me understand WHY he sees things as he does.

This is an intelligent, kind, thoughtful human being. He is not my enemy. He is not a white supremacist. He does not want a Civil War. In fact, I think, in the end, Jim wants the same things I want – peace and prosperity, justice and fair play and equity for all.

Maybe this is the one thing we can do for each other right now – instead of dehumanizing each other and seeing each other as "The Enemy" – maybe we can make an effort to "humanize" each other – to see the good in each other.

I want to thank my friend for letting me dialogue with him tonight

Cheryl G. writes*: I love this, Karen. It is so true. A dear friend of mine and I were talking about this very thing today.*

Thank you so much for trying to unite rather than divide, to help bring understanding, peace and love.

You made my heart happy!

Mary Ellen writes*: I love friendships like that, too.*

D writes*: Yes, that is what most of our side is all about. You may have your feelings and beliefs and it's ok. We just don't approve of the hate, violence, looting, etc. that left extremists are demonstrating.*

Karen writes*: If you meant to say that you don't approve of violence from the extreme left OR right then we are, of course, in agreement on this.*

November

Russian government-backed social media accounts nurtured the QAnon conspiracy theory in its infancy, earlier than previously reported, according to interviews with current and former Twitter executives and archives of tweets from suspended accounts...

The original posts associated with the QAnon conspiracy theory appeared in late October 2017, purporting to be from a Trump insider with "Q" security clearance who said Hillary Clinton faced arrest and her allies were running a massive child-sex ring.

The fantasy was confined to a small piece of the internet for a few days until conservative video blogger Tracy Diaz, known online as TracyBeanz, began to post regular videos promoting it. She soon began amassing undisclosed donors and now has more than 10 million video views on YouTube.

Menn, Joseph. "QAnon Received Earlier Boost from Russian Accounts on Twitter, Archives Show." Reuters, 2 November, 2020. (https://www.reuters.com/article/us-usa-election-qanon-cyber/qanon-received-earlier-boost-from-russian-accounts-on-twitter-archives-show-idUSKBN27I18I))

My Inner Rabble Gets Roused

I've now and then shared some of the thoughts that have brought me healing. Usually these are thoughts of hope and joy, humor and cheery positivity. But sometimes there's another mental place I go when I need healing – a place that I've been weirdly reluctant to share with others. But… maybe it's time. Here it is: Sometimes I just get completely angry and exasperated with sickness and gloom. Sometimes my inner rabble gets roused and I get this powerful sense of indignation towards anything that would try to foist itself on me that I don't want foisted on me. Sometimes I feel this powerful surge of revolt against anything that would try to take away my God-given right to wholeness and holiness. I laugh at the gloom, pull it from its fear-built pedestal, and knock it into smithereens. Yeah. Sometimes anger seems to work well for me. So there it is. My secret's out at last. Thanks for letting me make my confession. I feel so much better now.

Alrighty. Carry on then…

A Deck Full of Blessings

Sitting in a camp chair on the back deck
in the sunshine, I open my eyes and see
the answers to my "When will I ever…?"
questions: "When will I ever find my love?"
And there sits my beloved partner of 36 years.
"When will we ever have children?"
And there sits Xander, eating lunch.
"When will we ever own our own home?"
And I look down at the deck beneath my chair,
attached to our house at my back.
"When will we ever have another cat?"
And there's Clara Rose with her nose
between the slats of the deck, looking out
on our field of autumn auburn trees.
I am sitting on a deck full of blessings.
-Karen Molenaar Terrell

November 4, 2020

No matter who wins the presidential election, this won't change: There are still good people in the world doing good things. And you are one of them.

November 5, 2020

God bless our country. God bless the whole world. No matter who wins this election we still have a long road of healing ahead of us. May God, Love, help us all – each and every Republican, Democrat, Libertarian, Green Party, Black, Brown, White, polka-dotted, atheist, Christian, Muslim, Hindu, Buddhist, Jewish, gun-toting, unarmed, flag-waving, anthem-kneeling, F and M and LGBTQ one of us.

Amen.

November 6, 2020

I am inordinately proud of myself right now.

At the beginning of the summer I planted carrot seeds in a small planter box on my deck. I watched them sprout and grow and felt pretty good about myself and what had come from my seeds, but... then I kind of forgot about the carrots. Occasionally the dog would stick her snout in the planter box and go grazing and pull a carrot out for herself. Scott transplanted some of the sprouts to his garden when his own carrots weren't doing so well - and my carrot seedlings did really well for him. But. Yeah. I got caught up in other things and, for the most part, the carrots just sat in their box. Waiting. Until today.

Today I remembered them! I went out to the planter box and dug around and found a bunch of little carrots - still healthy and edible. I brought them inside, washed them off, and turned them into (drum roll) CARROT CAKE! (I used some apple sauce Scotty had made from his Gravensteins, too - we're living off the land, baby!)

November 7, 2020

Van Jones's words on CNN spoke to my heart this morning:
"Well, it's easier to be a parent this morning. It's easier to be a
dad. It's easier to tell your kids character matters… telling the
truth matters; being a good person matters. It's easier for a lot
of people. If you're a Muslim in this country you don't have to
worry if the president doesn't want you here. If you're an
immigrant you don't have to worry if the president is going to
be happy to have babies stashed away or send Dreamers back
for no reason… 'I can't breathe' – you know, that wasn't just
George Floyd, that was a lot of people that felt they couldn't
breathe… and you're going to the store and people who have
been afraid to show their racism are getting nastier and
nastier… and you spend so much of your life energy just trying
to hold it together. And this is a big deal for us just to be able
to get some peace…And the character of the country matters.
And being a good man matters…"

I am feeling incredible relief this morning. But…I also
recognize that we're not done. There's still a lot of work ahead
for all of us – red and blue and green and polka-dotted – to
bring equity and progress and healing to our country. The path
in front of us is not lined with roses and unicorns – and I am
already emotionally exhausted from the LAST four years. But I
guess we've all got to take a collective deep breath and gather
our strength and march on. The battle's not over until every last
person on our planet is free and safe.

November 9, 2020

I know I have friends who are feeling today what I was feeling
four years ago. Devastated. Terrified of what the future holds.
Sure that there must be some mistake. Wondering if it's all a
lie. Wondering if some miracle will change everything before
the new president gets sworn in. I guess I just wanted you to
know that I get it and I'm not going to judge you for whatever
it is you're feeling right now. And I'm not going to think less
of you if you're feeling scared.

I voted for Biden-Harris. I am relieved and happy they won.
But I find I'm not even tempted to gloat about it.

Everyone Blessed

The sun doesn't choose to rise
on some and not others.
Everyone's blessed.
-Karen Molenaar Terrell

Thank you for being my friend, Peggy. You were an example
to us all of how to live an honorable and courageous life. I miss
you already.

Just a Happy Old Bat

I'm no one's competition anymore –
and I'm so grateful I've moved past that.
Any youth and beauty I might have had before
brought me into a rivalry I was never good at.
Now I'm just a happy old bat!
-Karen Molenaar Terrell

Just Love, Love, Love

Can't reason with delusion; can't reason with error
Can't reason with illusion; can't reason with terror
Just love, love, love
We've all of us been there; we've ALL been insane
This time it's OUR turn to heal someone ELSE's pain
Just love, love, love
The battle's already won – that's the deal
No need to respond to a lie as if it's real
Just love, love, love
Don't respond with hate, or anger or fear
Give nothing for the rage to bounce off of –
'cept a cushy wall of kindness and cheer
Just love, love, love
– Karen Molenaar Terrell

November 13, 2020

I did not want to get out of bed today. It was dark and cold "out there." I figured I could just stay in bed all day. Who was going to stop me, right?

But here's what happened instead: I remembered I wanted to reach out to someone who'd just lost a loved one. So I got out of bed and printed out a photo to make a card. Went to the post office to mail it. Got back in the car and decided to go exploring. Drove towards Padilla Bay. Came upon a humongous branch across the road. Another car pulled off the road and young Elijah got out of the car. Without saying a word to each other, Elijah grabbed one end of the branch and I grabbed the other and, working as a team, Elijah and I moved the branch off the road. I drove on to the Padilla Bay dike parking lot. There was only one other car parked in the lot. When I got on the dike I realized WHY there was only one other car parked in the lot. IT WAS CRAZY WINDY OUT THERE!!! Huge gusts of wind pushed against me and almost knocked me off the path. IT WAS GREAT!!! Now I was awake, for sure.

Drove home. Made myself some avocado toast and cocoa. Put "Mary Poppins" on the television and surrounded myself in cozy memories of Moz and Dad and watching "Mary Poppins" with them as a young girl.

Getting out of bed was a good idea.

November 14, 2020

I was thinking about my friend, Peggy, this morning - thinking about all the things I loved/love about her. And it came to me that one of the MANY things I appreciated and loved about my friend, Peggy Bissell, was her forthrightness. She wasn't afraid to ask the tough questions. When I was running for school board last year, she and another dear friend, Wendy, just came right out and asked me - without beating around the bush - questions that made me realize there were concerns about my religious affiliation I hadn't even considered might be out there: How did I feel about schools requiring vaccinations? How about the rights of LGBTQ students? What were my thoughts about creationism and evolution? Should creationism be taught in public schools? Should evolution be taught in public schools?

I am SO grateful to these friends for giving me the opportunity to share my views and beliefs BEFORE they assumed they knew what my views and beliefs were. And I'm so grateful to them for letting me know that there were concerns - maybe rumors? - about me and about my religious beliefs. Neither one of these women engaged in gossip or hearsay or talked about people behind their backs. They came directly to me to find out how I felt and believed and thought. I so appreciated that.

November 19, 2020

Forgiveness. Forgiveness is something I've given a lot of
thought to over the years. At different times different thoughts
about forgiveness have been helpful to me. When I realized
that I should actually THANK people for gifting me with the
challenges that helped me grow – that was a huge step forward.
When I realized that to NOT forgive was hurting me more than
anyone else – that was another step. And this week I had
another epiphany about forgiveness – and, for me, this one was
HUGE.

There were a couple books I read recently that helped lead me
to my most recent revelation:

I've been re-reading Baroness Orczy's "Scarlet Pimpernel"
books. In one of the books –*I Will Repay*– one of the characters
says: "To understand is to forgive." Whoahhhh. That got my
thoughts going all kinds of interesting places. If we can
understand other people – feel empathy for them – we can
forgive them because we recognize in them our OWN human-
ness, right?

After I'd read a couple of the baroness's books, I felt the need
for a change in genre – I needed to exchange the blood and
muck of the French Revolution for something a little lighter.
Something with some humor. So I brought Christina Lauren's
latest romance, *In a Holidaze*, to my Kindle. It was the perfect
book for me right now! Funny and light and with a happy
ending – just the escape I needed at the end of 2020. And it
was in this book that I came upon another quote that I found

helpful in my pursuit of forgiveness: "All this time I've been upset with him for simply being exactly the person I always knew he was." Sheesh. It makes no sense to be angry at people just because they are human beings – with the same human flaws and foibles we ALL share. I mean – none of us is perfect. There isn't a single person on this planet who hasn't done something stupid/thoughtless/unkind at some point. Let's forgive others their faults, and let's forgive ourselves, too, while we're at it.

All the Collective Love of the Cosmos

Up before dawn, enveloped
in the dark, in the bubble
of my car, as I drive over
country roads, listening
to Mindy Jostyn sing
"Morning Song"and I feel
God
with me. Not as a corporeal
being. Not as a Matter-being.
Not just as Moz or Dad –
but as the power and presence
of all the collective Love
of the Cosmos. Loving me.
Wishing me into a new day.
-Karen Molenaar Terrell

Love Is Still Here

The fourth Thanksgiving
without Moz at our table,
the first without Dad and
the first without a turkey –
we went vegan this year.
We forged ahead, making
it up as we went – creating
new traditions: a yellow
and red pepper dish; a bowl
of mushrooms sauteed
in olive oil – which we used
as our gravy on the mashed
potatoes; Broccoli steamed
to a brilliant green; and orange
squash made for a colorful plate.

I was yearning for something
old to bring to the feast –
something from the past –
and remembered Aunt Junie's
dishes with the blue flowers
around the outside. Scott
reached up and pulled them
from the top shelf for me
and put them on the table.
Much looks different this year.
But this hasn't changed:
Love is still here.
-Karen Molenaar Terrell

November 26, 2020

Back on September 25th, I posted this:

To the dear anonymous someone who gifted me with a $20 credit at Sisters Espresso -

Thank you! Your kind gesture meant so much to me! I have no idea who you are - I don't know your religion, gender, politics, or age - and I LOVE that! You could be any of us - your kindness represents the best in all of us - and I'm not sure I can find the words to convey how much I needed to see that right now.

Bless you!
Karen

I now know who left me the gift card. It was given me by my dear friend, Peggy Bissell, who passed on two weeks ago. I am so touched by Peggy's gesture. Even as she was gathering her energy to transition from here to whatever comes next, she was thinking of others. And that is so typical of Peggy.

Dear friend, thank you.

You're Still Here!

Karen writes:
Dear Republican friends -

You're still here! Thank you for coming back! After our last discussion I wasn't sure I'd ever see you again! I've been blocked, unfriended and snoozed by a lot of friends in the last four years – and I get it and am not dissing anyone for doing that – my feelings aren't hurt or anything – but it says a lot about your character that you're still here.

Thank you.

Jim S. writes: *While we disagree I'm glad that you post what you think and believe. Stating your case makes us both smarter in a way and is the most fundamental of American values.*

Mary Ellen writes: *I find this post extremely kind and a spotlight on the quality of Karen's character. It's why, despite our differences, I adore her as a fellow human.*

A.D.W. writes: *And let me say, Congratulations for having the apparent victory.*

December

District officials on Monday denounced the violence that erupted in downtown Washington over the weekend, blaming many of the clashes on protesters who refuse to accept the presidential election results.

Police said the Proud Boys movement of white chauvinists amassed its largest gathering yet in the District and was met by anti-Trump counterprotesters who police said willingly engaged the group.

- Jackman, Tom. Duggan, Paul. Ann E. Marimow, Ann E. Hsu, Spencer S. "Proud Boys Sparked Violence Around Pro-Trump Rally, DC Officials Say." Washington Post, 14 December, 2020. (https://www.washingtonpost.com/local/public-safety/trump-rally-violence-proud-boys/2020/12/14/bf2f5826-3e26-11eb-8bc0-ae155bee4aff_story.html)

That Was Magic - Right There!

So I was watching a Christmas movie with magic wands and
sparkling spells on the Disney Channel ("Godmothered" - it
was pretty fun!) and it took place in Boston - and there were
people everywhere - not wearing masks - just, you know,
walking around, going about their business, chatting, smiling,
going into restaurants, having their hair done - and I had this
moment when the thought occurred to me that THAT was
magic - right there! - and we didn't even know it when we had
it!

Alrighty. Carry on then...

December 3, 2020

No, it is not alright to grab your guns and threaten the lives of election officials who are doing their jobs. If you think it's okay to use violence to put your candidate in the White House – if you think it's alright to start a Civil War because your candidate lost – if you think it's fine to go against the votes and wishes of the majority of your fellow citizens – then you are NOT a patriot. You are a bully. I have no respect for bullies.

December 4, 2020

Look! I got a haircut - with bangs and everything! Haven't had a haircut since before COVID.

T'was Two Weeks Afore Christmas 2020

T'was two weeks afore Christmas and all through Eff Bee
not a creature was stirring – not a they, he, or she
We were frozen in place – old traditions wiped out –
finding it hard to remember what it all was about

There'd be no parties this year; no off-line celebrations
(some of us contemplated months-long hibernations)
Some of us would be zooming, others face-timing
(those of us without working mics would be doing some
miming)

There were still cookies to bake and gifts to send out
but this year we'd be masked-up as we moved about
Gone were the handshakes, the hugs, and side kisses –
replaced with tapping elbows as we went about our business

And as we forged on – made what we could of twenty-twenty –
we began to unfreeze and realize there was still plenty
of beauty all around us – joy and peace and kindness
We saw that gratitude brings us Christmas and Love it is that
binds us
-Karen Molenaar Terrell

Christmas Doesn't Depend on a Who, When, or Where

Here's the beauty of it – the whole Christmas thing
You don't have to go anywhere to find it waiting
You don't have to be anyone special or rare
Christmas doesn't depend on a who, when, or where
You can be at the North Pole, or on the equator –
at the bottom of the deepest sea, or in a volcano's crater –
it might be mid-July or it might be December
but Christmas is right now if we only remember
to open our hearts wide to the love all around
to witness the beauty, and feel the good of love abound
-Karen Molenaar Terrell

December 10, 2020

Two my deer English teacher friends (and those who speak
Homonymese) –
Eye thought it mite bee nice two give ewe sum thing too play
with two-day. Sew eye give ewe a Christmas story:

Once upon a thyme inn a land far, far away, their lived a young
girl named Surely. Surely was a suite child and was all weighs
looking four opportunities too give two those around her.

Won mourning, as Surely walked down the rode into the town
of Bethlehem, she past the in they're and herd a we baby
crying inn the manger. Surely all weighs carried her drum set
with her (because who doesn't, write?) and – bee-ing the suite
child she was decided two play her drums fore the knew baby
buoy.

She maid quite a racquet, let me tell ewe. Pretty soon people
were paying her too stop. She gave the money too the baby's
parents, Merry and Joseph. Because she was thoughtful like
that.

The End.

December 13, 2020

Like last Christmas, this Christmas I did not want to kill any trees. I just don't have it in me anymore. So, like last year, Scott cut off an extra trunk growing on our redwood in the back field. Scott said we were actually saving the redwood by cutting off the extra trunk because if a wind came it would split that baby right down to the nubs. This tree has character. Or maybe… this tree IS a character… It fits right in with the family.

Hold on… I think I'll go put some Groucho glasses on it…

Christmas Right in Front of Me

Tenaciously trying to tug tattered
traditions into my December –
there WILL be jangling jarring carols
on my CD player!
there WILL be cheesy Christmas movies!
And then it suddenly hits me –
my real life is so much better than these
ridiculous stories of make-believe!

I'm missing out on the Christmassy
magic going on right now, in this moment,
when I'm spending my energies
and focusing what I see
on what came before instead
of what's right in front of me.
-Karen Molenaar Terrell

December 15, 2020

There's a story about my friend, Jack Arends, in the Huffington Post. I'd recognize that hat anywhere. Jack's friendship with the Molenaar family goes back more than 60 years - his mother worked in the same office as Dad - Jack's mom was pregnant with Jack at the same time as my mom was pregnant with me (I arrived on earth a couple months before him). Our families have shared both tragedies and celebrations over the years. Yesterday Jack was my hero:

A Washington state elector who has a terminal health issue broke down in tears Monday after casting his vote for President-elect Joe Biden, telling a local media outlet that being an elector is part of making his time left "count."

...A retired aviation industry analyst, Arends entered the floor of the state Senate in a wheelchair and wearing a brimmed cap reading "Play Nice." He took a less-than-subtle jab at Trump by bringing two Sharpie markers — the president's writing tool of choice on several headline-making occasions   - to cast his vote for Biden and Vice President-elect Kamala Harris.

Curtis M. Wong, Huffington Post, December 16 (https://www.huffpost.com/entry/washington-state-elector-tears-up-casting-biden-vote_n_5fda09f3e4b0f8a9ede54cc4)

December 16, 2020

Email message: Your PayPal account has been limited. We detect unauthorize person was accessed your PayPal account and make some purchase.

December 19, 2020

Andrew and Xander and their partners, Christina and Kyla, have been sheltering with us off and on during the pandemic. I feel so blessed during this time when so many people are isolated and separated from their loved ones to have these young people under our roof. They're been such a help while they're been here: they've taken turns cooking meals; chopping wood; cleaning the kitchen; doing laundry; taking the dog for a walk.

Yesterday Christina and Kyla and I had a Girls' Day Out. (With masks.)

We took a hike around Lake Padden; stopped at Haggen's to buy the makings of a Thai food feast for dinner; popped in at Paper Dreams gift shop for stocking stuffers; and then at Ovn Pizza for their magnifico vegan pizzas.

It was the most fun I've had in a long time.

Solstice Rain Patter-Tapping

Wrapped up cozy in a downpour
on this winter solstice day
Rain patter-tapping on my
bumbershoot as I slosh along the way

I feel Love reaching out –
ever-here, ever-there, everywhere –
embracing me in Her gentle calm.
What choice do I have but to share?

Home to dry clothes and a fire
in the wood stove. Soon a pie
in the oven – filling our home
with baked blueberry smells – my
contribution to the solstice feast
of peace.
-Karen Molenaar Terrell

Why Would I Choose?

Why would I choose bitterness
and deny myself the peace
of forgiveness?
Why would I choose anger
and deny myself the joy
of kindness?
Why would I choose hate
and deny myself
the healing presence of Love?
-Karen Molenaar Terrell

December 23, 2020

Love and a Sunrise

I went for a drive as the sun was rising this morning and
pondered the concept of Love. I put in a CD of Alison Krauss's
music, listened to her sing the Beatle's "I Will" – and let the
music lift me up into that magical place where there's no anger
or fear, enemies or hate – where all of creation knows nothing
but joy and good will. I brought back this poem...

If I open myself up to Love
I avail myself of all the power of Love –
the warm, healing presence of Love.

Love isn't some fragile thing.
It's not destructible.
It's not pretty in a Christmas tree
glass ornament way.
It's enduring, dependable;
as solid as a mother's lap;
as strong as a father's rescuing arms;
as beautiful as the sound of Beethoven's
"Joy"- indestructible, and perfect.

Love fills all space –
every corner, hole, and crevice –
the collective consciousness
of universal compassion and kindness
nurturing and reaching out to
the love in all of us.
And the love in all of us can't help
but respond.

And that's how we heal.
-Karen Molenaar Terrell

December 27, 2020

A year ago at this time I began to feel Daddy moving away
from us. He died three and a half weeks after Christmas - two
days before the first COVID case was reported in our state and
our nation. He had impeccable timing. It's been a strange time
for me in the last week. There are times when I feel a little lost
and I can't seem to get a handle on the state of our world - or
the state of myself, for that matter. There are moments, though
- glimmers - when I feel incredible good peeking through - like
stars shining through a hole in the clouds. Moments when I feel
a lightening in my heart.

On election night four years ago the voice told me to "trust" -
that "everything is happening as it needs to happen. Don't be
afraid."

I feel the promise unfolding. We're going to be okay. We
already are.

Trust. Fear not. Love, love, love.

Ben T. writes: *Thinking of you, Karen! I find strange moments
where I think of the timing of my own dad's passing, and I find
myself saying "I miss him, but I'm so glad he's not having to
deal with all of this." At the same time, I know he would have
handled the year in his own way. The selfish side of me wishes
him to still be here, while the more empathetic side of me is
glad he's not. Both sides of my little flip flop seem to stir up a
whole cocktail of emotions.*

I usually settle on this... Those who pass on before us show us something inherent in life. And that thing is that we will also walk down those same roads someday. Why should we fear to walk down a road that has been so well traveled by loved ones before us?

Twenty-Twenty

A-jumble, a-jabber, agog, and afeared
on the lookout for what might come next
a cacophony, a galumphing, a grinding of gears –
dragged us through it – Egads! What a year!

Everyone will have similes and metaphors galore
to express what this gem was for them:
Scorched earth; or icy slopes we slip-slided
down – not trusting each step that we took.
Some of us bided; some of us chided;
Some forged ahead by hook or by crook;
Some froze in shock and waited to be guided;
Some held on as their whole world shook;
And some could write an entire book.

Our twenty-twenty was not all bad
It brought its share of good, too, lad –
It brought us bright rainbows
It brought us brave heroes,
It showed us who we are and all we had.
-Karen Molenaar Terrell

Last Night's Nightmare

Okay, remember when our nightmares involved running away from bad guys - and we were all alone and it felt like we were running through deep water and weren't getting anywhere? And we opened our mouths to scream for help and no sound came out? Yeah.

So last night's nightmare? I found myself sitting in a packed theater full of happy, laughing people - every seat was occupied and we were all sitting right next to each other, shoulder-to-shoulder.

I woke up, horrified. No one was wearing a mask!

Alrighty. Carry on then...

Jeff Chase writes*: It's strange to think how intimate we all once were. I miss that.*

Karen writes*: Me, too.*

Dawn B. writes*: I was actually thinking about this yesterday. We have all become so acclimated to social isolation over the last year that we will actually need about six months to readjust. It is going to be almost as hard as going into quarantine was.*

Pam A. writes*: My husband and I have each had dreams like that. I dreamed I was in a crowded bar and realized I was unmasked and so was everyone else.*

Karen Troianello writes*: I also dream about masks.*

Cari Hornbein writes: *I had a similar dream a few weeks ago, but it took place at a conference. I remember being really happy to see friends and colleagues, but mortified no-one was wearing a mask! So relieved to wake up and realize it was 'just' a dream, but it made me realize the underlying stress about being out in public these days.*

Pamm F. writes: *Yes, just had one myself where I forgot to bring a mask & I was the only one in a room of people without one. The entire dream I was running around searching this strange house for a mask that might be laying around.*

Connie W. writes: *I can't even watch movies or old sitcoms where they are standing too close, no masks, breathing on each other- I have to stop and realize they were made pre-COVID.*

January

In the early morning hours of Nov. 4, 2020, President Donald Trump told possibly the most consequential falsehood of his life.

The lie was that he had been reelected by American voters to a second term, despite tens of millions of votes still outstanding and rapidly narrowing margins in key states such as Michigan and Pennsylvania...

What happened on Jan. 6 and in the days that followed spun directly out of the original falsity and its subsequent embellishment. Supporters stormed the Capitol, wrecking historic rooms, barely missing the chance to seize elected officials. President Trump was impeached by the House for inciting the riot. He now awaits a Senate trial on the charge, his Republican Party riven by the events, Democrats aghast and furious, and threats of further violence hanging in the air...

- Grier, Peter. "Truth, Lies, and Insurrection. How Falsehood Shakes Democracy." The Christian Science Monitor. January 15, 2021.
(https://www.csmonitor.com/Daily/2021/20210115/Truth-lies-and-insurrection.-How-falsehood-shakes-democracy)

Wouldn't That Be Lovely?

Here's what would be really cool, I think: If egos would take a back seat. If people weren't branded as the "winners" and the "losers" in every political machination. If it wasn't all about taking credit and laying blame. If regular people weren't treated as pawns. If it could just be about... you know... actually helping people - helping the homeless, the oppressed, and the vulnerable . Saving the environment. Doing the right thing. Being kind. Being honest. Being decent. Wouldn't that be lovely?

Alrighty. That is all. Carry on then...

January 1, 2021

We made it! I feel like we've all accomplished some major something just by surviving to 2021.

Last night as I was falling asleep I thought again of that one-star rating someone gave me for my audio book (that rating appears at the top of the page any time I google myself) and I came to terms with it. Sort of. I figured it was going to be there as long as I needed it to be there. I decided to be grateful for whatever lesson I need to learn from it. And then I thought bigger than that. When I die, I realized, none of any of that is going to matter – not the five stars, not the one star, not my name or my reputation or my popularity – that stuff – all of it – will soon be forgotten and in 50 years nobody will even remember "Karen Molenaar Terrell" was here. The one star and the five stars have nothing to do with who I really am – with my real identity as a child of the Cosmos. What WILL matter in 50 years is that I was kind while I was here, and honest. Even though my name won't be remembered, I figure any kindness I leave behind me will leave an impression – a ripple maybe – that will join all the other ripples of kindness and help bring our little boat of mankind to the shore in a wave of Love. (I know. I am so deep, right?)

So anyway – this morning – the first morning of 2021 – I googled me again (I cannot help myself – remember that scene in "Schitt's Creek" where Johnny asks a freaked-out Moira if she "googled" herself again?) and some kind someone had added a 5-star rating to my audio book! Bless their heart. That brings my audiobook up to three stars now. And – to be honest (and because I'm still human) – that feels a lot better than one star.

Thank you, kind person.

Susanne K. writes: Karen, I don't chime in too often on posts, but I feel as though I need to correct an impression here. Many days (and sometimes multiple times in a day) my husband Phil and I will remark to each other, "Did you see Karen's post?" What that means to us is there is something of value that we need to share, whether it be a unique idea, an insight, a kindness, a photo, or something provocative that elicits a response that we share and discuss. I have never been one to put much stock into star ratings, mainly because I want to make my own determinations about the value of something. But I don't want you to labor under a misguided notion about your value, at least in our household. I would bet there are many of us (a silent majority) who look forward with much anticipation to your posts. THANK you for all that you do for our communities, for the tone that you set and challenges you set for us.

Karen writes: Susanne, I read your comment and started crying. You filled a hole in my heart that I didn't even know was there. Thank you.

Taking Down the Christmas Tree

Taking down the Christmas tree
seemed especially hard for me
this year.
Every ornament brought back
memories – sweet and dear –
as I wrapped them up (both
the ornaments and the memories)
and packed them in the Christmas sack.

Ornaments Mom left me after she passed.
Ornaments from former students in my class.
Ornaments our sons made of pop-sickle sticks
and glitter, macaroni and beads.

I felt the loss.

And I know. I know. I know.
I know all the things you want to say:
I know that Good is never really gone-
It's here to stay
It lives on –
in our memories. I know Love never ends –
and I should be grateful for all the family,
all the friends,
all the love I've known in my life.

But as I take down the tree
I'm missing you especially.
-Karen Molenaar Terrell

January 3, 2021

Dear friend who's proudly showing off her new gas mask in preparation for her march in DC on January 6th:

Just curious - what do you think is going to happen there? Do you expect our legislators to set aside the legal votes of millions of American citizens because protesters don't like who those citizens voted for? Do you think this is the way a democratic-republic works?

These are strange and really surreal times....

The Awakening

Fear not. Feel the movement of the universe
endlessly adjusting, unfolding, winging like
a great murmuration of birds in flight – moving
as one body in waves of Love on winds of Truth,
winking and twinkling in the joy of the Cosmos.
Unwinding, untangling, unfettered and free-flowing-
always moving towards Love, towards Truth,
towards Life – irrepressible, unstoppable, the mighty
inexhaustible, relentless power of justice, of wisdom,
of kindness and peace. All of creation pulled together
and pulling together – The Awakening.

Amen.
-Karen Molenaar Terrell

January 4, 2021

So this picture of a mountain pops up on my screen - and I'm
thinking it's one of those photos that comes up when I turn on
my computer- pictures of exotic places around the world - and
I'm like - hey! That's Mount Baker! And what a great photo!
And then I realize that... it's MY photo... and I put it on there as
my screen saver months ago.

A couple of takeaways here:
- I'm a pretty good photographer.
- I'm losing my marbles.

January 5, 2021

2021 so far:

Day 1: Took the new year out for a spin on the Bellingham boardwalk.

Day 2: Padilla Bay dike trail.

Day 3: Squires Lake hike with Andrew and Christina.

Day 4: The power went out for an hour or so. We sat in serene stillness around the woodstove. A tea kettle heated atop it. Clara Kitty dozed on my lap. I watched the rain tapping on the deck outside the French doors. It was wonderful. And then the power came back on and that was okay, too.

Day 5: First physical healing of the New Year. I tripped and fell outside this morning and heard something snap in my ankle as I went down. There may have been some cussing. Pain so intense I felt I might throw up. Scotty came over and put out a hand and helped me get up. He helped me hobble over to the car - I had an appointment for my car today and was happy to find I could put pressure on my foot and drive without any problems. I prayed as I drove to the appointment - felt Love gathering me into Her arms. I felt enveloped in warmth. After the initial fall (and landing), I felt no pain at all. The only thing left of the whole experience is a swollen ankle. But I figure that's nature's way of keeping everything snug and in place, right?

And now we're watching Rick Steves traveling through Croatia
as the wood stove works away for us. And in a few minutes
we'll watch Alex Trebek as he appears in his last Jeopardy
week.

January 6, 2021

If you think intimidation, threats, and violence are acceptable ways to run a democracy, you are not a patriot; you are a bully. If you think it's alright to overturn an election that has been proven to be legitimate over and over and over again – by the courts, by security experts, and by state election officials of both parties – you are not a patriot; you are a sore loser. And if you think it's acceptable to encourage and incite violence to force your will on a nation of people who voted you out of office, you are not a patriot; you are a traitor.

***

Whoah. Trump has brought Republicans and Democrats together. I mean. Not in any way he intended. But still…

Last night I was wondering how this day would unfold - how we would make it through to the other side. I trusted it would work out somehow - but I couldn't imagine what would have to happen for the legislators to come together and do what they needed to do. And wow. I'm watching the electoral college certification on PBS right now – and I'm listening to the Democrats and Republicans who were under siege together today getting up, one after another, to unite together to support our Democratic process. I'm really inspired here. Giving praise to the irrepressible unfolding of Truth.

Here, again, is the message I got on election night four years ago as I looked up at the stars: "Trust. Everything is happening as it needs to happen. Don't be afraid. Trust."

***

A.D.W. writes: *Hi everyone. I am back from DC and, oh my gosh, what a day!!!*

I have so much to say but let me share most directly for now— that the stream is being cleansed and important stuff is going on. Our Republic will be stronger than ever if we proceed in faithful prayer and knowledge, and look beyond the narrative being spun right now. (Like all the other narratives we've had to endure for years — until more is known.)

January 8, 2021

My dear Humoristian hooligans –

The world is in need of all the love and courage you can shine on it today – the world is in need of your reflection of all that is good and decent. You are important – each and every beautiful one of you – in your expressions of kindness, honesty, and irrepressible, unstoppable, insurmountable joy. May the scared, misguided and misinformed be awakened by your unwavering wisdom and unshakable faith in Truth. May the bullies and belligerent bigots be transformed by your buoyant, unbreakable belief in the brotherhood and sisterhood and kinship of all creatures. May we all help our world find peace.
Amen.

– Karen

Checking in: Everyone okay out there?

Amanda B. writes: Good morning. I miss you soooo much! Doing fabulous over here! How are you doing?

Karen writes: How lovely to hear your voice this morning! We're still plugging away here. I'm a little surprised and delighted when I wake up each morning to discover I'm still here. I miss you, too. Give everyone there hugs from Karen, okay?

Amanda B. writes: I definitely will! I love your calendar - it is hung up for everyone to see. I definitely will give everyone a hug, but I can't wait to give you a big ol hug when this is all over!

Roland M. writes: *I am still moving, breathing, and farting. So, I must be doing fine. I hope you are doing similar.*

Susanne K. writes: *Just holding on for dear life, and taking solace in the natural world and my family. How about you, Karen?*

Karen writes: *Every new day I wake up - and find I'm still living in a democracy - seems like a miracle to me right now.*

Ruth R. writes: *Exhausted. It's been a long week.*

Elizabeth E. Fisher writes: *Bought my first small bunch of daffodils yesterday. Spring is on my table and on its way!*

Elly H. writes: *I started listening to your "madcap" book. Your voice lifted me up just when I needed it. Will continue book after work today. Thank you!*

Karen writes: *Thank you so much for sharing this, Elly!*

David B. writes: *So glad it's Friday!! And we're joyously prepping for our first Covid 19 vaccine clinic next Wednesday!!!*

Diana P. writes: *Good morning, Karen! Every morning I wake up I feel blessed - so it's all good here. I love that you have your brood there. It can be too quiet around here.*

Craig F. writes: *Yep. Beautiful snowy day here in NC.*

Karen writes: Wonderful! (We haven't had any snow here, yet - a nice covering of white would be nice.)

Mary B. writes: Fine on the Skagit. Getting out everyday and finding the joy. Went snowshoeing on Sauk yesterday.

Karen writes: Snowshoeing on Sauk sounds GREAT!!!

Todd S. writes: Rodger that! All clear!

Astrid A. writes: Best I can; best I can; I'm just trying to get along the best I can'.

Allen N. writes: OK. Which, when grading on a curve, is a "C." Passing. Don't quite dare to be "great."

Jeff Chase writes: Good morning! All is well. Glad to hear you are, too. Hoping your ankle is healing up. There's much to be grateful for. After all of the events of the week, I completely forgot the Seahawks will play their first playoff game against LA on Sunday! Happy Blue Friday!!

Karen writes: I know! I didn't know about the Saturday game until yesterday. Something to look forward to! This is going to sound weird - but I'm actually grateful for my experience with the ankle this week - it forced me to turn immediately to Love and trust in that power and feel the warmth and presence of my Father-Mother again. It sort of woke me up. The initial pain went away instantly as soon as I did that. Today the puffiness is almost completely gone and the bruising is fading - and I'm having no problems walking at all! Thank you for reminding me of the good that's been going on in my life this week!

Jeff Chase writes: I'm so glad you're mending well (and that you told me the game is tomorrow lol). Have a beautiful weekend!

Myra R. writes: Yes I am. And all whom I love!! Xo

Cyndi W. writes: Karen, I do look forward to your posts every day. I'm hanging in here, taking each day as it comes and am grateful to be healthy and alive!

Karen Rippberger writes: Yes. I've been confident for quite a while that error continues to be exposed and all will be well.

That is not to say there won't be strife and hardship for some in the meantime. There always is in times of adjustment—humanly. But chemicaluzation cannot hurt us.

Shawn M. writes: Present.

Cheryl G. writes: Just peeking in to say hi. Everything is wonderful. Nate is doing well. I am in Idaho with my other son and family.

Just want to say thank you, my friend. Thank you for being you.

Yes, Karen, it's all good here.

Barry M. writes: I'm waking up with a smile on my face again! It's been a few years.

Lori M. writes: Hanging in there, except it's frigg'n snowing in NC!

Mary Ann writes: Hugs.

Amando writes: Good to go.

Dawn B. writes: *It was a very long week, but spring is coming and hopefully we are through the worst of the political craziness*

Beverly C. writes: *Cold, but sunny for a change up here in PA.*

Janice M. writes: *Life continues well in our small corner of Bow. The churning in DC is disturbing. How do we close the divide in our nation? One person at a time.*

January 9, 2020

As we were awaiting January 6th - KNOWING what was
going to happen - my friends and I were reassuring ourselves
that if WE knew from our Facebook feeds what was coming,
surely the feds knew, right? They'd be prepared, we told each
other. We were shocked when we watched it play out on live
TV.

Kathy T. writes: Karen, exactly!

*Mary Beth writes: I have been so distressed emotionally that I
haven't been able to sleep very well for at least three months
because this is what I feared - it was just a gut feeling - I know
so many others, even politicians, are now saying they saw it
coming.*

*Karen A. writes: I had been watching CNN off and on to see if
the race was called for Ossoff. A friend and I decided to drive
to the "big" town to get Thai to celebrate the Georgia wins. A
half-hour later, we're a bit early to get our takeout, so sitting
in the car we checked the race, and got coup news instead. It
was surreal for both of us. Here our country was in the middle
of a coup, the capitol building is overrun and being looted,
lives are threatened and lost—and we were sitting in the car
waiting for takeout. And with all that going on, there was
nothing we could do but—get our takeout and go home and eat.
Of course I could pray. But it wasn't like we could somehow
defend the capitol or anything.*

Mostly what an attempted coup looks like is life as usual.

January 10, 2020

Andrew and Christina left today for another adventure. It's
been such a pleasure to have these two young people living
with us the last couple months. So grateful to have their
physical presence with us as long as we did, and so grateful for
the love that connects us wherever they go. This mama's heart
is full.

Loss Brings Love

Loss
teaches me there is no separation
in Love
there is no space between
Good and me
Loss shakes old beliefs
shakes off what is untrue
and makes me look at everything new
What's left is real
what's left is true

Love brings loss
Loss brings Love
– Karen Molenaar Terrell

January 14, 2021

Back on New Year's Eve 2015, I bought my little Ford Fiesta,
Rosalita Ipswich O'Molenovich. Today she reached 100,000
miles on the odometer. I found myself tearing up – thinking
back to all the adventures Rosalita and I have shared in the last
five years, and all the memories that are packed inside my little
car. Rosalita still has the red scrapes from all the times we
shoved Mom's red walker into her hatch. I can still picture my
centenarian father sitting in the passenger seat, his head turning
as he took in the scenes on our drives together. I remember the
adventure Dad and I had in Rosalita when we jostled over wild,
rutted roads to the Big Four Inn.

Thank you, Rosalita, for helping me care for my parents.
Thank you for helping me get Mom and Dad to doctor's
appointments, and epic celebrations. You've done well, little
one.

Karen: I need to make a 100,000 mile appointment for my
Ford Fiesta.
Friendly Mechanic: How about January 21st?
Karen: Yes! We'll have made it through the Inauguration by
then!
Friendly Mechanic: (Brightening) That's right! So if the world
hasn't caught on fire we'll plan to see you next Thursday?
Karen: Sounds good!

***

Xander and Kyla are in the process of opening a new vegan scone shop in Bellingham. Scotty and I have been lucky enough to be their taste-testers the last couple months - our bellies filled with scones and flatbread and vegan appetizers - and our home filled with the smells of yeasty baking things. I am a proud scone-grandma.

January 18, 2020

Went on a nice long walk in Bellingham this morning - needed the fresh air and space for my thoughts.

I reached out to Dad in my thoughts (I don't mean that I, like, "summoned" him - Dad's not a ghost or anything - he and Mom are always with me in the same way Love, God, is always with me). And the thought that came back to me was full of joy. I know Dad's happy. I think I was trying to talk to Dad about all the uncertainty and grief of these times - but it came to me that the things I seem to be experiencing are no part of Dad's experience - no part of "where" he is (and I don't mean "where" as in a location - but as a state of mind). I felt that I was being encouraged, then, to claim my own joy, too. The words from John came to me: "Your joy no man taketh from you."

I'm not sure I'm explaining any of this at all well, but... the gist of it is that what I've been learning, lately, is that whenever I feel like I have a hole in my heart - it's instantly filled with Love. Love is constantly giving me whatever it is I need. My sense of being connected to the infinite Love of the cosmos isn't dependent upon my parents or husband or children or friends - it's always with me.

January 19, 2020

Today was the anniversary of Dad's passing. And I realized today - as I was trying to conjure up again that moment when I learned he'd passed - that there's no need for me to relive the details of that day. No need to focus on his passing. Much more important to focus on the wonderful and amazing life he had here.

How blessed I was to have the parents I had.

January 20, 2020

Oh man. Lady Gaga (I don't think I've ever heard a more beautiful and heart-felt rendition of our anthem - my thoughts went back to what was happening there on January 6th and it gave our anthem a whole new meaning for me), and Klobuchar, JLo and Garth Brooks and Amanda Gorman made me teary – and that didn't surprise me, really. But I was really moved by Mike Pence's presence and Mitch McConnell's presentation of the flag to VP Harris – and… what the heck?! I never could have seen THAT coming. January sixth changed so much for our country – and not all of it was bad. In the end, people I never would have expected became heroes. Whoah.

I'm feeling proud to be American again

Soaking Up the Inspiration

My emotional, mental, spiritual be-ing
is absorbing the hope and joy of the new day
soaking up the inspiration like a thirsty tree
in a desert that hasn't seen rain for four years.
-Karen Molenaar Terrell

January 20, 2021: Today I Celebrate You

My dear Humoristian hooligans -

We're still here! We've lived through yesterday and made it to today and that has been no small feat.

Today I celebrate you - each and every beautiful one of you! I celebrate your compassion, courage, and commitment to kindness. I celebrate your honesty, your decency, your charity. I celebrate your moral strength and integrity. I celebrate that you stand for justice; kneel for equality and fairness; and dance for the joy that no one can steal from you.

You have transformed the world. You have made it a better place. You are a wonder.

A new day is dawning. Go out there and work your magic, my friends.
Karen

Bob S.A. writes: *I celebrate YOU, Karen; today I celebrate YOU!*

Karen writes: *Oh wow. I wasn't expecting this - this really touches me. Thank you, Bob.*

Bob S.A. writes: *Look in the mirror more often, me dear; you is GOLD!*

Karen writes: *Awww... you're bringing me tears this morning, my friend.*

Bob. S. A. writes: *Good.*

David B. writes: *I see the LIGHT!*

Jeff Chase writes: *What a day!! The work of spreading love and kindness is never done, but today our burden is lighter. I'm so happy to share this with you. Enjoy every minute.*

Karen writes: *We made it, little bro!*

Jeff Chase writes: *Yes, we did, sis! I'm so happy!*

Recalling Influential People Who Died in 2020

Dee Molenaar, 101.Celebrated Seattle mountaineer who was a National Park Service climbing ranger, geologist and artist. Jan 19.

The Seattle Times Staff and The Associated Press. "Final Goodbye: Recalling Influential People who Died in 2020." The Seattle Times, 31 December, 2020. (https://www.seattletimes.com/nation-world/final-goodbye-recalling-influential-people-who-died-in-2020/)

A Year and a Day

On the nineteenth of January my father died
And so began the roller coaster ride
that was 2020 and 20 days -
a year we struggled to find our way.

At first there were empty streets and quiet weeks
of smogless skies and distant peaks
I found peace in the stillness - peace in the calm
That time alone was a much-needed balm.

But after - a montage of images flashes
now through my mind -
much of it dark, some of it kind -
exploding up, crashing down,
fire and rage all around
Our nation boils and seethes
and a Black man gasps, "I can't breathe"

Veterans protect fathers with leaf blowers
who protect the mothers who protect our Black sons
and daughters from tasers and guns.
Ahmaud, Breonna, and George - say their names
Black Lives Matter - our nation sits in shame
as bigots and bullies scramble to shift the blame -
and settle on "Karen" (which is really lame).

And a just woman with a doily collar
and a selfish man who keeps up the holler
and lie of "Stop the steal"
and refuses to let the nation heal -
our neighbors reel and keel in their zeal -
fed rumors and news that are not real.

Dye runs down a lawyer's face
a narcissist screams, "Show your strength!"
NAZI and Civil War flags fly in our streets
D.C. police pummeled and beat.
Racism and bullying and bigotry and hate,
caskets of COVID victims, rioters climb gates
Long lines for vaccinations, as people wait.

In the end the heroes win - as heroes always do -
they step up and vote and stop the coup -
they wear masks to protect each other - me and you -
they stand up for Breonna and Ahmoud and George -
and in the fiery fire a stronger land is forged.
-Karen Molenaar Terrell